I'm Just an
Illinois Farm Boy

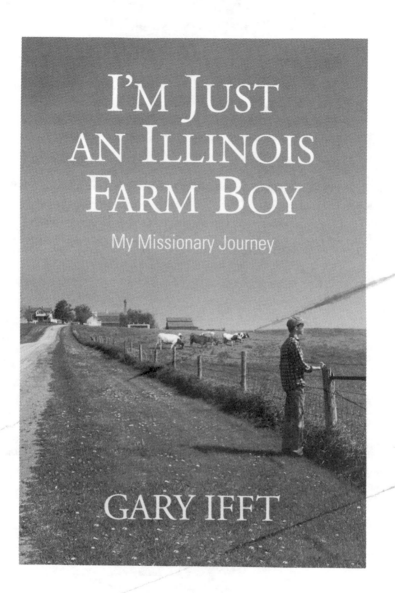

I'M JUST
AN ILLINOIS
FARM BOY

My Missionary Journey

GARY IFFT

Belleville, Ontario, Canada

I'M JUST AN ILLINOIS FARM BOY
Copyright © 2010, Gary Ifft

ISBN: 978-1-55452-456-3

To order additional copies, visit:
www.essencebookstore.com

For more information, please contact:
gary.peggyifft@yahoo.com

Guardian Books is an imprint of *Essence Publishing,* a Christian Book
Publisher dedicated to furthering the work of Christ through the written
word. For more information, contact:
20 Hanna Court, Belleville, Ontario, Canada K8P 5J2
Phone: 1-800-238-6376 • Fax: (613) 962-3055
E-mail: info@essence-publishing.com
Web site: www.essence-publishing.com

Printed in Canada
by

Guardian
BOOKS

Dedication

I am dedicating this book to my Uncle Melvin and Aunt Katherine Huber. They, along with their children, initially inspired me to become an overseas missionary and have been my lifelong examples and encouragers.

Contents

With Gratitude

Now that I have undergone (and survived) the writing and publishing of this, my first book, I understand the purpose of a section acknowledging those who helped bring it to fruition. It brings closure to the process of getting the book out into the public, and it gives me the opportunity to recognize people who have supported me in the process.

My first, and special, acknowledgment goes to my editor. Angela Reedy read much of the first draft and made many excellent suggestions. These suggestions led to a much improved second draft. The third draft resulted from suggestions I received at a Christian writer's conference that I attended with my editor. Angela reviewed the third draft in painstaking detail and pushed me relentlessly to improve my style, to "show, not tell," to drop adverbs, and to remove approximately 1,000 "thats" from the manuscript. The hours she spent on editing and proofreading my copy are too many to count.

Angela (she prefers Angie) is my daughter, our firstborn. Throughout her education, all the way through college, she, with great trepidation I am sure, gave me her papers to review. I marked them up liberally, and she probably wondered each time why she put herself through that punishment. My hope is that she recognized that she received better grades on her papers. From her childhood Angie has loved to write. After college she landed a job where she wrote and got paid for it. Motherhood called her away from that job, but she has since become a published author in the local newspaper with a regular column. She, as does her dad, also aspires to publish a book (or books) someday.

Secondly, Ron Walder, graphics designer par excellence, designed the cover of this book. Ron and his wife, Louise, are special friends and supporters of our ministry. His offer to squeeze the design of this book cover into his hectic schedule meant a lot to me, as I knew the product would be excellent. I gave him some ideas, a few instructions, and flew off to Ethiopia. The product you hold in your hands is what he did with the bare-bones concepts I gave him to work with.

Third, I personally contacted fourteen publishing houses about publishing this book before deciding on Essence Publishing in Canada. Writing a first book is a scary process with lots of strange terminology and unfamiliar industry practices. I needed someone to hold my hand. Many publishers do not seem to want to speak to the author. My phone calls to some publishers directed me through a voice-mail maze where each path ended up with directions to visit their Web site. I had already been to the Web site; now I wanted to talk to a person.

After first visiting Essence's Web site, I sent them an e-mail asking for more information. It seemed as though I had barely hit "send" when my phone rang, and it was Sherrill Brunton. Sherrill answered my many questions with patience. Each time I wrote she answered immediately. When I called I was able to speak directly to her rather than voice mail or listening to the recording telling me to visit their Web site. Because the editing, designing, and publishing would have to be done from far-away Ethiopia, Sherrill's offer to personally shepherd my book through her company won me over. Her personal touch convinced me to self-publish my book with Essence.

Fourth, I want to acknowledge the willingness of my bride, Peggy, to give me the time to write this book and the encouragement and support she provided. We have a very busy mission in Ethiopia, and I know it was difficult for her to watch me dedicate so many hours to this book when other tasks were screaming at us. She was patient with me, and she handled a lot of details and decisions while I labored over my laptop. Peggy, my lifelong companion and best friend, knew this book burned inside me begging to be released. Thank you, honey, for believing in me.

Peggy supported me in this book-writing adventure in a very special way by babysitting our two grandchildren while Angie and I attended the weeklong writer's conference. Angie and I spent from 8:00 a.m. to 9:00 p.m. in classes, at meals, and in discussions with writing professionals, while Peggy changed diapers, played store, and fed ducks.

And, finally, thanks be to God and our Lord Jesus Christ, for giving me the desire and ability to pursue the goal of being an overseas missionary. Although the path was long and winding, eventually we made it. It has been an extraordinary journey, and a blessed one. And thank You also for giving me the desire, talent, and perseverance to put that journey, and the accompanying message to aspiring missionaries, down on paper.

Gary Ifft
March 2010

Introduction

"Gary, I'm putting you on one-year probation from your position as administrator here at SIL, and Peggy, you are not invited back to your job as member services director after you return from your visit to the U.S."

With these crushing words from the director of SIL (as Wycliffe Bible Translators is known overseas) in Addis Ababa, Ethiopia, we felt like failures as missionaries, incapable of doing the work we had dreamed of for so long. Since early in our marriage in the late 1970s, Peggy and I dreamed about, prayed about, and planned on someday being overseas missionaries.

After pursuing many paths, with detours along the way, we finally arrived in Ethiopia in January 2001, bright-eyed and enthusiastic, naïve and ready to jump into the work God had so convincingly led us to.

Now, just over two years later, we sat sobbing in the presence of the director and his wife, the personnel manager, who had just shocked us by describing all the ways they believed we had failed.

I had always excelled in whatever I had undertaken. Be it in high school, college, graduate school, the U.S. Army, or employment in the corporate world, my performance was always exemplary. I regularly received the highest ratings and prided myself on my ability to do a good job.

For the first time in my life, I felt I had failed miserably.

In addition to the shock, Peggy and I were confused. Less than two months earlier we had received a letter from the chairman of the executive committee (the governing body of the SIL branch) promoting us to the status of being senior members of the branch. In this letter, he stated,

> We are very happy to have you as part of the Branch. We see that you are committed to the Branch's goals, as you both have demonstrated in various ways, and we are convinced that your contribution to the work here will make a difference. We appreciate your willingness to serve our Branch with its rich diversity of nationalities and personal backgrounds.

These accolades now echoed faintly from the past.

We were about to leave for the U.S. for our annual visit with our loved ones. Our daughter, Angie, was engaged to be married, and we looked forward to preparing for and celebrating the wedding while we were "home" in Illinois.

In addition, our son, Sam, who had been with us in Ethiopia, had recently enrolled in Rift Valley Academy in Kijabe, Kenya, and would be starting school there upon our return to Africa.

What were we to do now? Should we return to SIL after our vacation with these restrictions (my probation and Peggy's losing a major part of her responsibilities) hanging over our heads? What would Peggy do to occupy the balance of her time? Would I ever be able to satisfy the director enough to have the probation lifted from me? What would we tell our supporters, our family, our friends?

Little did we know that the director of SIL and his wife were dealing with some personal issues that made us the targets of their frustrations. We felt loved by all the other members of the branch and really didn't want to leave them. We had initially thought once we arrived at our assigned overseas post with Wycliffe Bible Translators, we would be there for the "rest of our lives."

But the message was clear—Peggy lost one major component of her work, and I would have to earn my position back from probation by jumping through a lot of hoops for the director.

Acting behind the scenes was God, who is always in control of all things. My perceived failure was the first step of an exciting new path for us in Ethiopia—a path we could never have come up with on our own. Little did we know that He had a much bigger, more interesting, and more rewarding journey planned for us.

CHAPTER 1

Missionary—
A New Word for Me

My cousin Luke Huber and I didn't get together often, as he and his family lived in Indiana, approximately four hours from my family's central Illinois livestock and grain farm.

However, Luke loved to visit our farm. The creek flowing through our farm provided a home to all kinds of wildlife—not only many fish, but also snakes, muskrats, raccoons, fox, pheasants, ducks, and more. Investigating the mysteries of that creek, as well as the entire farm, thrilled the explorer in Luke. He loved the outdoors and any kind of outdoors activity.

One day when we were around seven years old, Luke informed me, "Dad says our family is moving to Brazil."

"What is Brazil?" I asked.

"I don't know, but it's a long ways from here. We won't see each other very often any more, my dad says."

"Why are you moving to Brazil?"

"My dad says we are going to be missionaries."

"What is a missionary?"

Luke's leaving, Brazil, and missionary introduced heavy new concepts to my farm boy background. This is my first recollection of hearing anything about missionaries. Little did I realize how Luke's family's leaving for Brazil was to someday affect my own life.

The church denomination that I (and Luke) grew up in did not send out missionaries at that time. Our denomination was the Apostolic Christian Church of America, a conservative Anabaptist denomination. As a matter of fact, any church member who wished to pursue a missionary calling was likely to be excommunicated. Or else they voluntarily gave up their membership. A decision to go off to a foreign mission field had to be made very carefully, especially if one desired to stay within the denomination.

The Apostolic Christian Church (known by its German name Gemeinschaft der Evangelisch Taufgesinnten in Europe) was founded by Samuel Heinrich Froehlich in the early 1830s in Switzerland. He and his followers established churches all over Europe, with locations stretching from France to Ukraine.

Their missionary zeal brought the denomination across the Atlantic Ocean to America, and the church soon spread over a large part of the farming belt of the Midwest and beyond. In English the denomination name became Apostolic Christian. Apostolic Christian congregations can now be found scattered from the Atlantic to the Pacific, including some in Canada and Mexico.

As the years passed, the Apostolic Christian Church became somewhat withdrawn into itself, to the point where it reversed its stand on sending missionaries. Anyone wanting to become a missionary or itinerant evangelist had to leave the denomination. Fortunately, today the denomination is completing the remainder of a 360 degree circle and is once again sending out missionaries, domestic and foreign.

Peggy and I were both raised in this denomination. Some of our great-grandparents brought this faith with them from Germany and Switzerland when they immigrated to the United States. Our grandparents and parents were raised in the Apostolic Christian Church, found their spouses there, and continued to raise their own children, including us, in the church. It is a wonderful, warm, family-centered denomination that teaches biblical truth. But it did struggle with the concept of missions.

The ripple effect that Luke's Apostolic Christian family started by their decision to follow God's call to Brazil reached far and wide. Sending their son and brother and his family off to far-away Brazil was a very sad and heartrending experience for my Grandma and Grandpa Huber and his sisters (of which my mom was one). I knew I would miss Luke and my other cousins. I just didn't understand it all that much.

Luke's parents, Uncle Melvin and Aunt Katherine, did everything wrong according to today's missionary-sending standards and guidelines when they went to Brazil. But at least they had worked as domestic missionaries in Alabama for several years prior to leaving for Brazil. That experience gave them some introduction to the sacrifices and challenges of missionary life on the domestic front.

However, they had never been to Brazil before. They didn't know Portuguese. They had no mission-sending organization. They didn't have the full support of any church denomination, although their local church in Indiana did give them its prayer support. They weren't familiar with the Brazilian culture. Their family would have to be financially self-supporting.

And, on top of that, when they were about to leave Miami on their long flight to Rio de Janeiro with three young children, Aunt Katherine went into labor. She delivered their fourth child, Becky, in Miami, and their departure was delayed, but for less than two months. They were eager to get to Brazil, even with a newborn baby.

Over the years my family received many letters and sets of slides from Melvin and Katherine, telling of their work. These letters and slides described the churches they planted and the people who had come to know Jesus through their ministry. Their lives sounded so intriguing, with their completely different lifestyle and different foods, pets, houses, schools, etc., I wanted to trade my farm pets for a monkey like they had. While my cousins learned Portuguese and attended boarding schools, my central Illinois farm boy life seemed quite lackluster in comparison.

Uncle Melvin's family left for Brazil in February 1956. Unfortunately, no one from the Huber side of the family visited them until around 1980, when some of my aunts and uncles went to see them. Perhaps it was the long flight, perhaps the logistics, or perhaps the expense. Peggy and I and our two oldest children (Angie, five, and Becky, two) were next to visit in 1982, but that's another story...

I will come back to this family, which had so much influence in my life, later on in this book. However, I have introduced them at this point to explain my first contact with the concept of "missions" and "missionaries." Little did I realize at that point in my life that I was actually way ahead of my friends with my familiarity with missions. I had real, live missionary uncle, aunt, and cousins who lived in the faraway country of Brazil. And their obedience to God's direction in their lives was going to impact the direction of my life.

CHAPTER 2

Haiti

Growing up isolated out on the farm undoubtedly stimulated my desire to see a bigger part of the world. That desire was probably enhanced by some latent wanderlust passed down from my great-grandparents, who emigrated from Europe. It definitely was not Ifft wanderlust, because when my father and mother married, they moved just around the corner from the farmstead my dad grew up on. They lived on that farm from 1946 until 1989, when they retired from farming and made a major move seven miles north to the small town of Fairbury.

Throughout my childhood we didn't travel at all. Our only vacations consisted of one weekend at Wisconsin Dells and one weekend in St. Louis, each about three hours away from home. When I was nineteen, I went with some young men from our church on a fishing trip to Ontario, Canada, and then on west to Saskatchewan. That was the first real vacation of my life, and I was thrilled to go to a "foreign country."

For taking that trip I received the reward of staying home and taking care of the farm and livestock while the rest of my family went on the first ever family vacation more than one state away from Illinois. They went to see my aunt and uncle who lived in Colorado Springs. I had seen the Rocky Mountains on the way back from Saskatchewan, or otherwise I would have been very envious of their seeing mountains without me.

After I graduated from the University of Illinois in 1970 with a bachelor's degree in chemistry, my travels picked up. I was drafted into the U.S. Army during the height of the Vietnam War. President Nixon couldn't wait to get his hands on me, as I received my draft notice the month after I graduated. Other than going to the state of Washington for reception into the army, I spent my entire army career in Texas at two different forts. At Ft. Sam Houston in San Antonio I received basic training and medical laboratory technician training. Following that I was shipped to Ft. Hood, three hours away in the desolate hill country of Texas, to work in the laboratory at the large Darnall Army Hospital. I served there until the end of my draft commitment of nearly two years. I had a strong desire to travel while in the army, but the desire was not so great as to cause me to want to travel to Southeast Asia!

I had the opportunity to visit several more states in the next few years as I became independent of my family; however, my next big adventure was going to Florida for our honeymoon in 1975.

Peggy Rager and I both grew up in the Apostolic Christian Church, she in western Ohio and I in central Illinois. In our denomination young members of the church do not date, but rather participate in group social events. Over the years we saw each other occasionally at some of these events, such as weddings or baptisms.

In 1973-74 both Peggy and I attended Purdue University in West Lafayette, Indiana. That is where we started to get to know each other better. I was studying for my Master's of Science in Industrial Administration (which was Purdue's equivalent of an MBA), determined to get that degree in one year. After discharge from the army I had worked for a year as a research chemist. Sensing that I would not advance with my employer without a PhD in chemistry or an MBA, I decided to go to school to get the master's degree.

Peggy studied dietetics in the College of Home Economics. Because of my heavy course load, I essentially had no social life, although I did see Peggy on a few occasions. At that point Cupid had not yet shot his arrow.

Prior to graduation from the MSIA program I was hired to work at the corporate headquarters of State Farm Insurance in Bloomington, Illinois. State Farm offered me a six-month internship prior to my move to Bloomington at any of its twenty-five regional offices in the United States or Canada. I could have gone to California, Oregon, Arizona, Florida, or any of several other appealing locations. However, as I looked over State Farm's list of regional offices, I saw they had one right there in West Lafayette. After the rigors I had been through with course pressure and studying day and night, it seemed most convenient not to have to face a move across the country. Some days I questioned the wisdom of that decision, as I thought of the missed opportunity to experience an almost risk-free six months stay at any of several attractive cities around the U.S. But God had other plans for me.

Working for State Farm was a lot less time-consuming than my graduate studies had been. I re-entered social life. More and more I became attracted to Peggy. I was twenty-five years old and felt the time had come to marry and begin a family. Eventually the Lord clearly showed me as a result of my prayers that she was to be my wife. Following the procedure practiced in our denomination I asked for her hand in marriage through the elder of my local church. Upon my asking, he wrote a letter to the elder of Peggy's church, who subsequently told Peggy's father. Following that, Peggy's dad told her I had asked her to marry me. She responded with a "yes" back through those same channels.

After the positive answer came back, our engagement was announced on Sunday, November 17, 1974, in both our churches. We were married on a cold, sleeting February 16, 1975, in Peggy's family's church near the little town of Latty, Ohio. I was blessed not only with a wonderful like-minded wife, but also a great, loving family. Peggy is the middle of seven children, all of whom, along with their spouses, love the Lord. Being part of the Rager family (and their in-laws) has been a special blessing to me over all these subsequent years.

These life events primed me for the next opportunity that God sent my way. By 1980 I was anxious to see an even bigger part of the world than the United States and Canada. Peggy and I were at my parents' home one evening, and they asked if we had heard that my Uncle John Fehr planned to visit Haiti. This seemed like such an interesting adventure that I ached to go too immediately upon hearing about it. I wondered why I shouldn't experience this trip along with Uncle John.

That evening I called Donald Steidinger, a neighbor to my parents and the organizer of the trip to Haiti. I had worked for Donald and his brothers for two summers shelling corn—where we took his big corn-shelling rig to neighbor farmers' corncribs and spent long, hard days at the arduous task of emptying their corncribs and turning ears of corn into truckloads of shelled corn.

Such days were times of bonding, and through them Donald and I became good friends. So when I called him, he warmly greeted me. He told me, yes, there was one place left on the airplane. Donald and his father, Urban, both had a long-term desire to visit a young Haitian pastor, Esaie Dieudonne, whom they had gotten to know from his visit to their family many years earlier. Esaie became an evangelist in Haiti, and the Steidinger family supported him in his work. In order to make the trip to Haiti, they hired a Christian farmer pilot, Dean Pusey, who took groups of interested Christians to the island in his small airplane. Dean considered introducing people to the material and spiritual poverty of Haiti one of his life's missions.

I had no idea (and neither did Donald) how rigorous a trip it was to fly from Bloomington, Illinois, to Port-au-Prince, Haiti, in a cramped six-seater Piper Aztec plane. The men on the trip, in addition to the pilot, were Donald, Urban, Earl Steffen, my Uncle John, and me.

On a cold January 1980 day we met at the Bloomington airport around lunchtime, packed the plane, submitted our flight plan, and took off south. After a stop to refuel, we flew to St. Petersburg, Florida, and stayed at a very basic YMCA guest house.

We had a system of each passenger taking a turn saying a prayer for safe travel before we took off each time. The next morning, as we prepared to depart St. Petersburg, it was my turn to pray over the next leg of the journey.

After I said "Amen," Dean engaged the starter for the engine, but it refused to turn over. After some examination we learned that the starter bendix was burned out. It took several hours to locate a new bendix and replace it. When the plane was finally fixed and we had climbed in again, I noticed Dean didn't call on anyone else to pray for our trip, but rather he himself prayed for a safe journey.

Donald and Earl were large men. Because we had such a small plane and a lot of weight, we were required to pack light. Dean wanted most of the weight in the front, so Urban and I, being the two smallest, had to crawl over the seats and luggage each time to get to our seats in the back. Before that trip I thought I knew our Steidinger neighbors fairly well. However, by spending all those hours in the back seat of the plane with Urban, I learned a lot more. His seventy-five years of life experience, seventy-five grandchildren, and more great-grandchildren than he could probably count provided many hours of entertaining stories for my benefit.

We flew out over the Atlantic, and I had a soaring realization that I had broken free of the North American continent for the first time in my life. This experience fanned the flames of my passion for international adventure.

We landed in the Bahamas for fuel, and even there I saw an entirely different culture and lifestyle. Nearly everyone was black, and the demeanor of the people appeared to be much more relaxed. I sensed no urgency among the airport attendants to fuel our plane for the final leg of our flight to Haiti.

Esaie Dieudonne met us at the Port-au-Prince airport. He arranged for us to visit many different missions and outreaches in Haiti to show us the ministries he was involved with. One of the most important items on his agenda was for us to meet several North American missionaries. We could sense his pleasure as he explained how those cross-cultural servants worked to improve the economic and spiritual life of his fellow citizens.

One evening while waiting for supper at one of the mission-aries' homes, the missionary mentioned that the transmission had gone out on his four-wheel-drive vehicle. When Donald heard that, he heard something he understood. The challenge of keeping all of his farm machinery and corn-shelling equipment running had made him a very skilled mechanic. Since he knew me well, he called to me to give him a hand.

As I mentioned, Donald was a big man. Before he left on the trip, his wife had told him that since his tummy was tugging on the buttons of his shirt, he should always wear a tie to cover where his shirt gapped in front. I found myself lying on my back on the ground next to Donald underneath the Land Rover, with Donald still sporting his white shirt and tie.

We unbolted the transmission, dropped it out, and appeared for supper somewhat worse for wear. Donald apologized profusely for showing up with oil all over his shirt and tie.

We had many enriching experiences in Haiti, but the ministry and lifestyle of the missionaries left me with a lasting impression. I could see that potentially this life of sacrifice and service was for me. I couldn't fathom what dedication it took for those men and women to leave their comfortable surroundings in the U.S.,

Canada, and Europe and live lives devoted to helping others and spreading God's Word to those who hadn't heard it before. It seemed to me to be the perfect display of Jesus' command for us to go out into all the world, making disciples for Him.

As I spent time with them, I began thinking about what it would take for Peggy and me to sell our home and possessions and move to Haiti as full-time missionaries. Little did I realize then that God was planting seeds. That trip was a small step down the path God would lead us on until we found ourselves also serving as missionaries in a foreign country.

To prepare for this, my first big overseas journey, I had read everything I could get my hands on about Haiti. There was no Internet or Google in 1980, so I pored over encyclopedias and books to learn everything I could about this interesting country.

During the many hours I spent in my cramped seat in the rear of the airplane with Urban, I mentioned, "You know, since we're going to be in Haiti, I sure would like to see a voodoo ceremony. I've read so much about them."

Urban looked at me in shock and exclaimed, "Gary, since we're Christians, we should have nothing to do with that!"

Humbled, and reminded of his seventy-five years of wisdom compared to my mere thirty-one, I settled back and didn't mention "voodoo" again. But we didn't have to look hard to find this aspect of the Haitian culture.

One day our team visited a small mud-hut church in a rural area. We heard a hubbub of voices and activity on the other side of the hedge next to the church and went around to the other side to investigate. Under a shade tree on a small farmstead was an old woman grinding grain with a large mortar and pestle. She was sweating under the hot sun, wiping her wrinkled forehead with the back of her skinny black arm. Urban had great compassion for her. He constantly battled a desire to give money to the poor people, yet pilot Dean and the missionaries repeatedly told him sternly not to do so. They knew that giving money in this indiscriminate manner would only make the Haitians think of money whenever they saw a white person.

But Urban pleaded with them, and finally they permitted him to give the old woman a dollar. He walked over to the woman, gave her a dollar, and said something like, "Jesus loves you," although, of course she couldn't understand a word he said. When she received the dollar, she exclaimed the Creole equivalent of "God bless you!" When her statement was translated to him, Urban thought, Oh, she's a Christian, and reached into his pocket and gave her another dollar.

At that point she became so excited she started shouting and dancing and singing. Others, especially the children, came over and joined her in her celebration. It became almost a riot, out of control. The missionaries quickly escorted us to our cars, and we took off.

Urban anxiously asked, "What happened?"

"Well, due to the excitement of getting two dollars, the woman and her friends worked themselves into a voodoo frenzy," replied one of the missionaries.

Much to his credit, after a short time Urban turned to me and said, "Gary, I told you that we shouldn't have anything to do with this voodoo, and here I paid two dollars to see it. Please forgive me."

On that trip, Urban and Donald Steidinger achieved their long-time dream of seeing Esaie and his work. It was very fulfilling for them, and they left blessed by all they witnessed. For some of my traveling companions the experience closed a chapter in their lives, but it began a whole new book for me.

I went home and related to Peggy my experiences and told her I felt touched and impressed by the missionary life and that someday I wanted to do that too. Not having experienced Haiti with me, she didn't understand my feelings and new dreams. She could sense something new and different had come over me and that I had changed, but she didn't grasp it. I wanted her to understand how I felt, but until she could see missionary life, feel it, taste it, hear it, and smell it for herself, it was going to be difficult to convey to her my changed heart.

CHAPTER 3

Brazil

Although not outwardly evident, God had begun turning Peggy's heart to missions. In the late 1970s our friends Roy and Ann Maurer invited us to attend a Wycliffe Associates banquet. Wycliffe Associates is a support organization for Wycliffe Bible Translators. At their banquets Wycliffe Associates not only serves a good meal but also provides an opportunity for an overseas Wycliffe Bible Translators missionary to speak about his or her work and the work of Wycliffe in general.

We regularly attended the Wycliffe banquets, and their presentations always deeply touched Peggy. Like me, Peggy grew up on a farm, sheltered from a lot of what was going on in the world. Discovering that millions of people around the world didn't have a Bible in their language shocked her. She realized that something she took for granted, God's Word in the language of her heart, was not a privilege shared by everyone on earth. She always left the Wycliffe banquets heavily burdened for those many unfortunate souls. Although she couldn't relate to my change of heart from my 1980 visit to Haiti, God had already begun preparing her heart.

After my cousin Luke Huber married Christine and had a couple of daughters, he and his family moved from where his parents were working in southern Brazil to the Amazon River basin. They moved to the unevangelized raw jungle town of Santarém, about 500 miles (850 kilometers) upstream from the mouth of the Amazon. Full of adventure and wildlife, this part of Brazil epitomized all Luke craved. He and Christine began sowing the seeds of the gospel. They started one church, then two, then three. And many churches continue to sprout from those seeds even today.

When Luke visited us on his trips back to the U.S., he always implored us to come to Brazil and help him. Being the adventurous, extroverted sort of man he was, desks and offices and budgets weren't part of his lifestyle. His style included boating up and down the Amazon, spearfishing for meals, and hacking his way into the jungle to reach still another village for Jesus. He was perfectly at home living off the land in the wilds of the Amazon.

He needed a director, an office manager, to handle the administrative details of his growing PAZ (Project AmaZon—paz means "peace" in Portuguese) Mission. With my MBA and office and management experience at State Farm, he saw me as the person who could provide that organizational and administrative capability for PAZ. He repeatedly told us, "The fields are white unto harvest, but we just don't have enough people and resources to reach all those who are begging us to come and share the gospel of Jesus Christ with them." His plea deeply convicted Peggy and me.

As passion for foreign missions grew in our hearts, Peggy and I both decided it would be good to visit the Hubers' work in Brazil and see if there was potential there for us. We committed to visiting Santarém in July and August 1982 with our daughters, Angie (five) and Becky (two). We stayed a month.

The airline tickets for the four of us were very expensive. They were $1,365 each, which is the equivalent of $3,000 at the time this book is being written. However, we figured this was that once-in-a-lifetime opportunity to see real foreign missions up close, so we dug deep and paid.

I know angels surround us on a daily basis and are always available to serve us. But my first experience in which I truly knew an angel was involved occurred upon our arrival by plane at Santarém.

The cheapest way to fly to Santarém from the U.S. was by Suriname Airways. The flight was very long, as we stopped on the Caribbean island of Curaçao, then in Suriname, then in Belém, Brazil (at the mouth of the Amazon), and finally in Santarém. We landed in Santarém around midnight. Since political relations between Suriname and Brazil were not good, the airport tower ordered our plane to park on the tarmac far from the terminal—probably at least one-half mile away. Our girls were very tired, so Peggy and I had to carry them, along with our carry-on luggage, to the terminal.

Slowed by our twelve pieces of luggage and our two exhausted daughters, we were dead last in line to pass through immigration and customs. While we waited we struck up a conversation with the man in line ahead of us. We asked a lot of questions about life in Brazil.

When it was finally our turn to pass through customs, the agent asked what was in all those boxes and suitcases. We told him they contained our personal goods and gifts for the church. He immediately ordered us to open all the boxes for his examination.

My heart sank.

There were so many pieces of luggage, my body ached from exhaustion, the girls were grumpy and crying, and there were some very expensive things in that luggage. I questioned why opening our luggage was necessary, and the customs agent simply repeated his order to open everything.

Just as I was about to begin tearing tape off the first box, the man we had talked to in line showed up again and asked what the problem was. After I explained that the customs agent wanted to see the contents of each piece of luggage, the man spoke something to the agent in Portuguese. The agent turned to us and told us to go on out, without having to open anything. I don't know what was said, but I realized later it was "God's angel" who cleared the way. To me that was a small sign of God's smiling down upon the purpose of our visit.

It seemed difficult to even breathe in sweltering Santarém. The stifling air and high humidity caused us to sweat without any exertion. We had packed several fans in our luggage, without which we may not have survived the heat. At that time I was a dedicated runner, always preparing for the next 10K race. I continued to run while in Brazil, but when I went out to run at any time except early in the morning the sweat ran down my face in rivulets for thirty minutes afterwards.

The best way to get around in the Amazon jungle was by boat on the network of rivers. Luke started a boat factory, manufacturing metal boats instead of the wooden boats the natives had used since the beginning of time. The metal boats were superior to the wooden boats in that the wooden boats were subject to rot and each year had to be taken out of the water for weeks to be recaulked and made ready for the next season of service. Luke gave the native missionaries metal boats outfitted with small diesel engines, so they could easily ply the waters of the Amazon and its tributaries to evangelize the villages along the banks. Many of those villages had never before had a gospel witness.

A lot of my work involved helping Luke at the boat shop. It was so hot that perspiration started to flow just at the thought of working. Getting down in cramped, claustrophobic places inside a boat really tested my character. I think I passed the test, but barely.

We saw the blessings of working as a foreign missionary along with the challenges. We traveled with Luke and his family on a three-and-a-half-day boat trip on the Amazon River. When we docked near a village the people would run and welcome us with open arms. It was so simple to share the gospel of Jesus as people sat at rapt attention to listen. For those isolated villagers this truly was "good news."

While on the boat, Luke provided our meals simply by taking his spear gun, diving into the river, and returning fifteen minutes later with enough fish for us to cook over a fire on the beach. ("Eat the piranha before they eat you!" was a slogan of his.) The river's current rocked us in our hammocks each night. Startlingly loud jungle noises of monkeys screeching, crocodile splashes, and parrot calls regularly disturbed our sleep. During those long night hours I struggled in my mind to know what place missions should have in my life. "Is the steaming jungle of the Amazon basin where God wants me and my family?" I asked myself over and over.

Evidence of growth of the PAZ churches surrounded us. Two of their most prominent churches in Santarém were being remodeled and expanded because of the need for more space to contain overflowing congregations. The PAZ church looks to cell groups for its growth. These group meetings, usually held in members' homes, are where the real discipleship and fellowship of the church take place. Cell group members feel comfortable inviting their neighbors and friends to a home, which is a lot less intimidating setting for them than the church. When the cell groups grow to a certain size, perhaps twenty-five members, they divide (or "multiply" in PAZ terminology) into two groups. They appoint a new leader, and more and more lost souls are brought into God's kingdom.

In our conservative denominational background, Peggy and I were both taught that public prayers (including mealtime prayers) should always be given by a man. At one meal Luke asked Peggy to give thanks for the meal. She almost fell out of her chair. But she did pray, hesitatingly, but well. From that day forward in our family, we always took turns among all family members to say the mealtime prayers, starting from the time they were just old enough to formulate a prayer. It has been a blessing to our family, and I think it instilled in our children the idea that any prayer, uttered in either the most simple or the most elegantly flowing words, is heard by God. Nothing is too small for Him to care about.

While in Santarém we learned life could easily be more simple than the lifestyle we lived back home in the U.S. And by not worrying about acquiring and maintaining so many material possessions, life is less stressful and more rewarding.

Even though our month of living in Brazil changed our lives, our experience did not convince us to move there. In our hearts, God seemed to be telling us the timing and circumstances weren't right. We were extremely blessed by the work of Melvin and Katherine (who had also moved up from southern Brazil to Santarém) and our cousins. We continued to pray for them and support them financially, but we decided a move to Brazil at that time was not right for us.

CHAPTER 4

Haiti, Again!

Our family experience in Brazil left Peggy eager to experience more of foreign missions herself. One cold winter evening in early 1984 we attended a Worldteam Associates banquet. We knew some missionaries who were serving with Worldteam and others who were very active with Worldteam Associates, so we tried to attend their banquets each year. Worldteam Associates, as with Wycliffe Associates, existed to support the primary missionary-sending organization.

After a stirring presentation regarding the need for volunteers on work teams, the various work team leaders dispersed to different parts of the meeting hall. Those of us interested in volunteering went to talk to the leaders for the area of the world we were interested in. If it seemed like a match, they wrote down our names as potential volunteers.

Since I had been to Haiti and wanted Peggy to experience it also, we joined the Haiti group headed by Ed and Shirley Hauter. Because of the many names signed up on their list we felt it was almost fruitless for us to sign up also. But we did.

A few weeks later, Ed called and asked, "Are you guys still interested in going to Haiti with a work team?"

We replied, "Yes, but we're surprised there's any room available for us. There were so many signed up."

Ed, in turn, surprised us by saying, "Everyone else has backed out. You two are the only names left on the list. If you don't go, I guess there won't be a team going to Haiti this year."

Peggy called a couple of her brothers, and through them and their contacts we soon had a full complement for the work team. Our project was to put a roof on a new church for Pastor Odoine in his small village of Zanglais. The new church was necessary to replace the small building his congregation had outgrown.

At that time our denomination had a policy forbidding participating with other denominations in "spiritual work" and discouraged "co-mingling of the faiths." While the Apostolic Christian Church had progressed to the point of supporting a World Relief Committee that oversaw "approved" or "sanctioned" physical and material projects like building schools and drilling wells, building a church, preaching, or evangelizing was still forbidden.

Except for Ed and Shirley, who actually were former Apostolic Christians, all members of our Haiti work team were members of our denomination. But since our project was to build a church—a spiritual activity—it was considered "non-sanctioned." That meant we received no financial support from our church. We had to come up with not only the money to fly to Haiti and for room and board but also for all the materials and associated costs to build the roof. Even with those constraints, fundraising was not difficult. Each team member contributed what he could. For the remainder, some members of the Apostolic Christian Church saw past the restrictions on spiritual activities and contributed.

Upon our arrival we found we were blessed with guest house accommodations in an idyllic location on a mountainside facing a beautiful white sandy beach and the azure ocean. Haitians aren't so fond of lying around on the beach and basking in the sun, so we had the entire wonderful beach to ourselves.

Unfortunately, the guest house was set up for the men to sleep in one half of the building and the women in the other, each half being a large open room containing several bunk beds. A cement block wall separated the two rooms. Since we were all married, it seemed a little harsh to be placed into such a romantic setting with spouses separated from each other. There were rumors of midnight rendezvous down at the beach.

Being typical American short-term missionaries (i.e., task-oriented), we felt driven to complete the large roof project in our one-week stint. We couldn't believe it when we discovered that one end of the building measured thirty-two feet wide and the other end thirty-three feet. We were going to have to build a roof for a trapezoid-shaped church! That meant every truss had to be built to a different length. So, instead of just making a pattern truss and reproducing it, each one had to be reengineered.

By mid-week we saw we could meet our goal of finishing the roof project by the end of the week. Then came the news that broke our hearts—at least the men's hearts. A long-time Worldteam missionary felt it would be great if we spent our final days in Haiti participating in a marriage seminar. We were all happily married couples (and all are still married to the same spouses yet today), but a marriage seminar was foisted upon us, whether we wanted it or not.

For the last couple of precious days we men looked longingly down the mountain into the village of Zanglais at that roof as we participated in conversations about our feelings and relationships. None of us men will ever forget that. During the rest of the week we worked evenings and every available minute to finish the roof. We were determined to finish what we came for. Before we left, we did have the opportunity to sit together under that roof with our Haitian brothers and sisters to worship.

Following that trip Peggy had now experienced Haiti and could better understand how it changed my life four years prior. She could understand why I came home a changed person. With this trip following so closely upon the heels of our trip to Brazil, the desire to become overseas missionaries within both of us was strengthened. But, as with Brazil, we did not feel God's specific leading to Haiti or that kind of mission work.

CHAPTER 5

Eastern Europe

Most of us have wondered at some time or other how different our lives would have been if we would not have met that one person, had missed that one conversation, had showed up ten minutes later, hadn't gone out of the way to do that one thing, had made that one investment, or some other seemingly minor variation in our day-to-day choices. Our lives would have gone down a completely different path; we would have married someone else; we would have been a plumber instead of an accountant; we would live in Vermont instead of Ohio; or any of literally a million different outcomes could have resulted to drastically alter the courses of our lives.

In a conversation in 1984 with my friend Bill Baumgartner, I mentioned that someday I wanted to travel behind the iron curtain and visit the churches of our denomination in those countries. Most people would have thought I was crazy, but fortunately not Bill and his wife, Jan.

As newlyweds, Bill and Jan had spent a summer in Switzerland. They worked on a farm and traveled around Europe on the weekends. During that summer they traveled to Budapest, Hungary, but now they wanted to return and go deeper into the Soviet bloc to visit the more difficult to reach churches of our denomination. Those eastern European churches were fruits of the labors of Samuel Froehlich (the founder of the Apostolic Christian Church) and his followers some 150 years before.

In 1984, the Soviet Union, consisting of Russia and its many satellite republics, firmly embraced communism. The Cyrillic letters CCCP, standing for the Union of Soviet Socialist Republics in Russian, struck fear into the hearts of people at events around the world from the Olympic Games to war games. The USSR taunted the West, and Nikita Khrushchev threatened the United States in the forum of the United Nations, shouting, "We will bury you." There was a space race and a nuclear race, and the threat of war between the superpowers hung over the world.

It would still be a few years yet before President Reagan would tell the general secretary of the Communist Party and president of the Soviet Union, "Mr. Gorbachev, tear down this wall," referring to the Berlin Wall, a glaring symbol of the divide between West and East, between freedom and tyranny.

It was during that time of the communist threat to the free world that Bill and I agreed if the opportunity ever arose, we would travel together behind the iron curtain to visit the persecuted churches. No one from our denomination had visited the churches in Ukraine, Romania, Czechoslovakia (now Czech Republic and Slovakia), and Bulgaria for years. Occasionally someone reported on visiting the churches in Hungary or Yugoslavia, which were easier to enter and travel within.

In reality, we didn't expect that door to ever open. But, as God has revealed many times over, He has a sense of humor. One day several months after our initial conversation, Bill called to ask, "Are you guys still interested in going to Eastern Europe? If so, we have someone who will take her vacation time and travel with us to all of the countries we want to visit, even including going inside the Soviet Union. She knows about six languages and is excited about doing this with us."

Jolan Szabados, a member of our church in Budapest,

Hungary, had visited Bill and Jan's home church in Bluffton, Indiana, and they became well acquainted. Together they began to plan a trip to Eastern Europe. The commitment I had made previously to go to Eastern Europe, when it seemed so unlikely, was a different story now that it could become reality. But I was still pumped up to go and not about to back down.

When word leaked out that we were planning to visit all those communist countries, we received a lot of discouraging comments. "Why would you ever want to subject yourselves to those dictatorial, dangerous countries? Especially when there is no compelling reason to do so?"

That just made us more determined to go. If it became reality, the trip would be the adventure of a lifetime—for us four Americans to enter those Marxist countries for the specific purpose of worshipping with our fellow brothers and sisters in Christ. These were the people who were suffering real persecution for their faith.

Some naysayers predicted that we, as Americans, would never get visas to enter some of the countries, especially Romania, Bulgaria, and the Soviet Union. Ignoring them, we dutifully sent off the application forms, passport pictures, and dollars to the Czechoslovakia, Hungary, Yugoslavia, and Romania embassies and consulates. Each one returned our passports with our visas stamped in them!

"Well, you'll never get a visa for Bulgaria—that's one tough country!" they said. Again ignoring their comments, we sent in our applications, and back came the visas from the Bulgarian Consulate.

Only one challenge remained—the Soviet Union! We had to go to a specially-designated travel agent in Chicago to submit our visa applications. Then the waiting, breath-holding, finger-crossing, and prayers for Soviet visas began in earnest.

We waited and waited, occasionally calling the Chicago travel agent.

Nothing.

The day before we were to leave on our long-awaited trip we still had no passports and no Soviet visas. Would the entire trip and all our planning fall through because we didn't have our passports?

After a call to the travel agent on that final day, we found our visas had just arrived at their office. Since we were leaving from O'Hare, we made arrangements to stop by their downtown Chicago office the next day on our way to the airport. We learned that cutting it close was the Soviet style. God not only has a sense of humor, but He also likes to test our faith and patience.

Upon landing in Frankfurt, Germany, we obtained a car and wended our way east to Budapest, Hungary, through southern Germany and Austria. After arriving in Budapest, we became completely lost and had no idea how to find Jolan's apartment. Nothing seemed to fit the directions we were given. Wandering around aimlessly for a long time, we eventually did the very American thing of stopping and asking a policeman.

Knowing no Hungarian, all we could do was show him Jolan's address written on a piece of paper. He tried to tell us how to get to her address, but it was just impossible to communicate. The four of us invited him to hop into our car. We gave him some candy and treats, and he very much seemed to enjoy our company. What we did not anticipate was the shock of Jolan and her apartment-mate as we pulled up to their home with a policeman.

It wasn't possible for us to understand the level of fear the normal Hungarian citizen had of soldiers and policemen. We found out later that on many occasions the Hungarian Christians preferred to stop and ask directions of a young child rather than asking a policeman or even another adult.

Westerners will never truly grasp the conditions the people living under communism endured, nor the way the government controlled them and instilled fear into their lives. The anxiety never left them; they never were able to rid themselves of the fears and dread of communism and those who governed.

Hungary was the most "free" of all the Soviet countries we visited. Without any restrictions we were able to go to church on Sunday morning. However, when the congregational singing began, the ushers got up and closed the windows to keep the sound of the hymns from being heard outside. Even though church assemblies were tolerated, I think they didn't want to push their freedom too far.

When we visited the rural church of Dunavesce in Hungary, the congregation overflowed to outside the church building, and the singing was loud and public. And unlike Budapest, the worshippers showed no apparent concern about being heard by outsiders. My guess is the local officials in the countryside didn't follow the party line as closely as those in the capital. During our time in Hungary we rarely felt watched or followed.

The people we visited in Hungary, especially those from the churches, welcomed us with open arms and warm hospitality. This, our first exposure to life under communism, revealed none of the steely coldness of Soviet citizens and hatred of America we had read about in the media. Instead, we found friendly people who just wanted to live in peace, raise their children to be educated and productive, go to work, make a living, and enjoy the fruits of their labors.

After a few days in Hungary we drove to the Czech border. The crossing took a very long time, stretching from afternoon into the evening. Our patient driver, knowing that all four of us knew some German, however, muttered over and over, "Amerikaner kompliziert machen." (Americans complicate things.)

After crossing the border, we visited a home where we were treated to a very large meal and gracious hospitality. At about 7 p.m., as we were wrapping up the feast, our hosts announced that a congregation about two hours away was expecting us. We had had a stressful day of traveling and border crossing. I calculated that if we left immediately, drove two hours there, fellowshipped with them for even one hour, and drove two hours back, it would be midnight by the time we returned. I wasn't ready to face that after a stressful day.

Our hosts went off to call that distant congregation. "The Americans won't be coming to visit your congregation. It's too late. They are tired, and it's a long trip to your village."

"Okay, but we're sadly disappointed. We want to meet them so badly. Our entire congregation has been waiting at church since 8 this morning."

Upon hearing that, we decided we had no choice but to buck up, forget our own comforts, and do the right thing. We piled back into our car, visited with the congregation, and returned well after midnight. I was humbled for having dragged my feet about going. The Czechoslovakians hardly ever had visitors, and never visitors from America. It meant so much to them that we came all the way from the United States to visit them and listen to their stories describing the circumstances of their lives.

After spending a few days in Czechoslovakia, we returned to Budapest, where we boarded a train to Kiev, Ukraine. At that time Ukraine did not have its own identity as a nation. It was merely part of the Soviet Union. Our anxiety level notched upward, as this was a time of great apprehension for us. No one knew for sure how Americans would be treated when trying to enter and travel within the Soviet Union.

Ten members of the churches of Hungary traveled with us. At the train station the elder of the Budapest church came to give me greetings and other messages to convey to the elder of the church in Ukraine. While he was doing so I noticed on the platform a very suspicious suitcase, which was wrapped in black tape and tied up with cords.

We later found out that was a decoy suitcase. One of the

Hungarians had placed three Bibles in another suitcase that looked like it belonged to an ordinary tourist. In addition, he had prepared the suspicious-looking suitcase, with only clothes and personal goods inside, to attract attention. He boarded the train with both suitcases.

The Hungarians were not officially allowed to be in the same train car as us Americans, although both parties later discovered we could covertly visit back and forth in our respective compartments. All four of us Americans squeezed into a tiny compartment containing two benches facing each other. The benches served as beds, and two bunks folded down from the wall above. Under each of the benches was storage space for luggage. We hardly had room to turn around, and our knees bumped the person sitting across from us. It's a good thing we were friends.

Crossing the Soviet Union-Hungarian border took a long time. First, the Hungarian soldiers came through and inspected all our documents and every piece of our luggage to make sure all was in order. We had just let out a big sigh of relief over "passing inspection" when again we heard a sharp knock on our compartment door. We protested that we had already been inspected. But we learned that this time it was the Soviet soldiers demanding to check everything all over again. So much for Russian-Hungarian trust of each other.

It was not comfortable to open our suitcases in such cramped quarters and was a real inconvenience to dig all that stuff out once again. The soldiers again searched every square centimeter of everything we had. Our National Geographic magazines intrigued them the most. Apparently, in their drab culture, they didn't often get to see such colorful publications.

After we passengers had been inspected by both sets of soldiers, we felt the strange sensation of our car being jacked up. Since it was 2:00 a.m., when I looked out the window the only lights I could see were lights being used by crews changing the chassis wheels on our train. I could see the workers jacking up the train cars on the track next to ours, which confirmed to me they were raising up our car also.

This extremely intriguing activity outweighed all the other unusual events of crossing the border. All the wheels on all the train cars had to be changed. The rail gauge (distance between the rails) of the Soviet tracks was 5 feet (152.4 centimeters). The gauge of the European tracks was 4 feet 8 inches (148.5 centimeters). We understood they were purposely made this way to keep the Europeans from invading Russia by simply driving their trains in.

If United States and Canadian railroad track gauges were of different widths, the travelers would simply transfer to a different train at the border and continue their journey. But after all the security measures we had been through at this border, the Soviets apparently couldn't risk allowing us passengers to go outside and transfer to a different train. They simply locked the doors to the train cars and the doors to the toilets. The toilets drained directly onto the tracks, so by locking the toilet doors the authorities prevented us from dropping things (notes, money) onto the tracks.

There were dual tracks in this border station—European and Russian. The workers unbolted all the European wheel chassis from all the cars and rolled them out one end of the train. From the other end they brought in new wheel chassis designed to fit the Soviet tracks. They let the cars back down on the new chassis, bolted them on, and we were good to go. We entered the station on European tracks, and we left on Russian tracks.

Security was extremely tight at the border. At one point I put my camera up against the window to take a picture (without the flash, of course) of this amazing wheel-changing procedure, as I figured no one would believe that things like this actually happened. Immediately a soldier slammed the butt of his rifle against my window, shouting, "Nyet, nyet" ("No, no" in Russian).

About an hour or so after we resumed our journey into Ukraine, Jolan sneaked over to our compartment, overcome with excitement. Although both the Hungarian and Soviet soldiers had searched their luggage, neither had asked them to open the plain suitcase containing the three Bibles. However, they had insisted the suspicious looking suitcase wrapped with tape and twine be opened, only to find clothes and other personal items. Our group had successfully smuggled three Bibles into the daunting Soviet Union.

During the twenty-four-hour train trip to Kiev we learned a lot about how the people of Ukraine (the Soviet Union) lived. What we saw out the window as we traveled the hundreds of miles to Kiev did not indicate a mighty power that could "crush" the United States. The circumstances of the people visible to us seemed to indicate they were eking out a living bordering upon poverty. The people and all their surroundings were drab, colorless, and void of enthusiasm.

We found more surprises at the train station in Kiev. As I stepped down from the train, a man who appeared to be expecting us asked in excellent English if I were Mr. Baumgartner. I told him that I was not but Mr. Baumgartner was just behind me. The man, seeming to want to be helpful (but probably to make sure we didn't go off on our own), took one of our suitcases and hurried us off to the front of the train station, where only one taxi waited—ours. We were not allowed to interact with our Hungarian traveling companions at the train station. We heard later that our Ukrainian hosts had been sitting on a bench as we passed by, but fear of the authorities kept them from introducing themselves and welcoming us.

The taxi driver whisked us off to the nicest hotel in Kiev, the Dnipro. The mighty Dnieper River, from which the hotel receives its name, flows through Kiev. The ground floor of the hotel served as reception and restaurant. The hotel manager assigned us rooms on either side of the elevator on the second floor. For twenty-four hours a day, an employee sat at a little desk making sure we signed in and out each time we left, taking our keys when we left and giving them back when we returned. The hotel staff was aware of our every move, as we also had to declare our destination when we left.

We Americans stayed at one hotel, the Hungarians at another, and the Ukrainians who we had come to meet were at a third.

The Soviet Inturist agency assigned a guide to accompany us everywhere we went. Our Ukrainian guides did not allow us to enter each other's hotels. Fortunately, we did have some prearranged signals allowing us to stay in touch with each other and plan our clandestine meetings. That meant that on many of our outings our first order of business was to lose our guide so we could walk around independently.

The guides strictly told us that our visa allowed travel within only thirty kilometers (twenty miles) of the city center. That rule prevented us from trying to go to the town of Ossetia, the location of our denomination's church. Because of our travel restrictions, four members of that church risked a lot, including possibly their lives or freedom, to come to Kiev to meet with us.

This was the first time in anyone's memory that any American Apostolic Christian Church members visited the churches of our denomination inside the Soviet Union. We could not have possibly explained to them that this visit had come about simply as a challenge between Bill and me a year earlier. Our Ukrainian hosts had a difficult time trying to figure us out. We were not elders, ministers, or any type of leaders of the church, but simply rank-and-file members with a strong interest in them and their circumstances.

But, bottom line, that made no difference to them. They felt overwhelmed that believers from America, the great land of the free, remembered them and had made the huge effort to visit and encourage them. It didn't matter that we weren't elders of the church; it only mattered that we, brothers and sisters in Jesus Christ, cared about them and shared a common faith.

On a couple of occasions they told us this visit was so significant to them that they were willing to go to prison, if necessary, just for the opportunity to meet with us. After those meetings, we four Americans looked at each other and confessed we weren't ready to go to a Soviet prison because of meeting with Ukrainian friends.

Delivering the gifts we brought for our hosts presented a challenge. We couldn't enter each other's hotels, and we certainly couldn't just hand them gifts on the street. We devised a plan for Peggy to carry a bag full of gifts out of the hotel each day. One of our Ukrainian hosts would meet us with an empty bag. She and Peggy would sit down beside each other at a restaurant or in a park. When they stood up, they simply took each other's bag.

The next day we filled the empty bag that Peggy had picked up, and at the designated meeting the ladies again discreetly exchanged bags. We did this until all the gifts were delivered.

An American friend of ours wanted to send some gifts to the people of the Ukraine church. She told us she had placed several packs of Kent 100 cigarettes at the bottom of her bag of gifts. Being Christians, we didn't think it would be good for us to carry cigarettes. But she strongly urged us to take them, as we might never know when they would come in handy.

Sure enough, we found out that Kent 100s were more valuable than hard currency in the Soviet Empire. As an example, as we prepared for the return train trip to Budapest we asked some restaurant workers to prepare sandwiches and Pepsis for us. They showed no interest in doing so. Coming from the communist culture, they lacked motivation to provide good customer service. They simply didn't feel like preparing our lunch for us. After we told them there would be a reward of three or four packs of Kent 100s, they quickly began work. Within moments we had our sandwiches and soda.

Each of the five days we were in Ukraine we met, through some covert means or other (e.g., by taking a walk in the woods or visiting a communist monument), with the Hungarian and Ukrainian brothers and sisters. One day we went to a park with an outdoor amphitheater. There we sang hymns in three languages from our Apostolic Christian hymn book, which the churches in all three countries share. Those types of moments are what the Ukrainians said they were willing to go to prison for. We Americans didn't have that same level of dedication. However, our Lord watched over all of us and spared us from any harm. The significance of those outdoor sing-a-longs didn't hit us until much later.

At the end of our time in Kiev we reboarded the train, crossed the border with the same inspections and chassis changing, and returned to Budapest. This time we headed south from Budapest towards Romania. We picked up another Hungarian translator, a young sister in the church named Eva Szabo. After worshiping in her church at Dunavesce and spending time with her family, we traveled on to the Romanian border.

Just before we got to the border one of our Hungarian hosts, driving his own car, stopped us next to a wheat field and told us to wait as he drove on alone to a wooded area. We could see him at a distance working underneath his car. When he came back, we took off again. Later we found out he had somehow hidden a box of Bibles under his car, which the border guards did not catch. He passed over the border in the Warsaw Pact lane and got through with a much less intense inspection than we endured.

It's hard to imagine now, in the 21st century, some twenty years after the fall of the Berlin Wall, how precious the Holy Bible was to the people of the communist countries. And it's also hard to fathom the risks outsiders took to smuggle Bibles into them. This often reminds me how precious the Word of God is and challenges me not to take its availability for granted.

Crossing the border into Romania took six and a half hours. We could see our Romanian hosts on the other side of the border, but being in the Western citizen's lane meant every square inch of our car, including underneath, had to be searched by the border guards and their dogs. We waved to our as-of-that-time yet unintroduced friends across the border, but we were unable to communicate to them our extremely long anticipated waiting time.

At the crossing all Westerners were required to pay ten U.S. dollars per person per day for their intended length of stay in the country. Maneuvering through that bureaucracy also held up the line for a long time. In addition, at the border we were allowed to buy hard currency gasoline vouchers. Our Hungarian hosts strongly advised us to buy them, and we found that purchase to be exceedingly valuable later.

In Romania, as in all the communist countries we visited, reporting in to the police immediately after entering was our first order of business. We were required to submit our entire itinerary for their country. At each hotel the management collected our passports and reported our presence to the police. Staying in private homes was not possible. Even if we stayed at someone's house until late in the evening, and even if they had plenty of room for us, we were not allowed to stay overnight with them. We always had to stay at a hotel so that our travels could be monitored.

In Romania, where we felt watched and followed all the time, we visited quite a few families and some of our denomination's underground churches. One of the Romanian elders built a room inside his house with no windows to the outside. It was in this cramped room that they conducted church services with as many people present as could be squeezed in.

Late one evening we visited a sister in her apartment. When the conversation got too loud or someone laughed, she put her finger to her mouth and hushed us, pointing to the walls, indicating the presence of listening ears on the other side.

We heard the all-too-familiar stories of family members and friends reporting each other to the communist authorities. Our friends strictly warned us not do anything to arouse suspicion or bring attention to ourselves or them.

At one point our car's gas gauge was showing empty, and we desperately needed to find one of the few fuel stations in the country. When we thought we could go no farther, we came upon a line snaking its way into one of the stations. Our hearts leapt with joy and then, just as quickly, sank. Our Hungarian friends inquired and learned it was a "three-day" line. That meant once you entered the line you waited three days to get to the pump. We didn't have that kind of time.

We saw ropes tied between the cars in line to keep other cars from butting in. Every so often during the day the car owners returned to the line to push their cars ahead by hand as the line inched its way toward the station. From the end of the line, we literally could not see the station.

However, we discovered those fuel coupons we had purchased at the border with hard currency allowed us to go to the head of the line. We gave the attendant our voucher, and he waved us to the pump. Our fuel tank could not even hold all the fuel it allowed us to buy, so the attendant asked if we had jerry cans, bottles, or anything else to put the extra fuel in. We didn't. As we exited the station a man with tears in his eyes and an empty shampoo bottle in his hand asked us to siphon out enough gasoline to help him get to a place he desperately needed to go to—I think it may have been a funeral. We did.

Can you imagine the riot that would erupt in the United States if our cars were in line for three days to buy a few liters of rationed fuel and a Romanian could drive to the head of the line, have his tank completely filled, and even be asked if he had a container to take away more? I hate to think about the consequences; however, at the time we were extremely grateful for that opportunity.

After about four or five days visiting Romania, we set out for Bulgaria, a country we had been strongly advised against visiting. In spite of some seasoned travelers telling us getting visas for Bulgaria would be impossible, we had gotten them. We were determined to enter the country and take advantage of our visas. Our observation was that in Bulgaria Westerners were the least welcome of all the countries we visited.

After another long and challenging border crossing we found ourselves in a very poor country. No one in our group spoke Bulgarian, making every move a challenge. We ended up always having to find an intermediary, for example, someone who spoke Russian, since we had a few Russian speakers with us. The conversations went from Bulgarian to Russian to English and back again.

Four very old ladies made up the entire remnant of our denomination's Bulgarian church. One of our objectives was to find the village where three of the elderly ladies lived together in one house. After driving through the countryside inhabited by many poor people and rundown houses and around and through large flocks of sheep, we found their house. Communication with them was nearly impossible, so we wandered around their gardens and often just sat and looked at each other.

Eventually, we decided we probably had stayed there long enough and prepared to leave. It was then we discovered a problem with the old Russian Lada driven by four young men from Hungary who had accompanied us. All the grease in the front left tire wheel bearing had gotten hot, melted, and ran down the tire onto the ground. They couldn't drive their car, as the wheel would get hot and bind up after only a short distance without grease.

The aged women knew nothing about cars. It was late Friday afternoon, and businesses had started to close for the weekend. No one knew of any garage or car mechanic in the area. The nearest town was miles away.

We needed to be in Yugoslavia for church on Sunday, and the chance of our making it on time looked dismal. All of us uttered some kind of prayer for rescue.

As we sat pondering our fate, I saw a man walking down a path through the grass toward us. As he neared me, he asked in German, "Was ist los?" (What is wrong?) I explained to him about the wheel bearing problem and our dilemma of needing to be in Yugoslavia the day after tomorrow.

He replied, "No problem; I have wheel bearing grease in my car."

I was amazed—how many people carry cans of wheel bearing grease in their cars, especially these days?

I asked him to hop into our car, and I drove him to his car—a shiny new Mercedes-Benz—in a little nearby village. He reached under the front seat and brought out two cans of wheel bearing grease. We went back to the old Lada, packed the bearing, and took off with the grease for future packings.

At that point we parted ways with our Hungarian friends. The boys drove back to Hungary, and we headed toward Yugoslavia. Later we heard from them that they never had another problem with that wheel all the way back to Budapest. Truly God had sent us another angel, one who spoke German and delivered premium quality wheel bearing grease straight from heaven!

We experienced the most mysterious event of our entire trip when we visited the fourth old woman in her tiny apartment in another little village.

We drove and drove through more flocks of sheep, over hills, and through several towns and finally arrived at the woman's village. After asking directions several times, we finally found her small apartment on the third floor of a nondescript building. After initial introductions we sat down to eat at a table crammed into her living room.

Her phone rang. The person on the phone wanted to speak to me! Since I didn't speak any Bulgarian, I tried my best to handle the conversation through translators.

Calling me was the hotel we had checked out of earlier in the day. They demanded that I come back immediately. I told them we were far away and could not possibly return to their hotel. We finished the conversation (or so I thought).

Immediately the phone rang again; it was the same hotel calling, and again they demanded I return to their hotel. Again I refused.

After one or two more calls, we came to understand that when I exchanged dollars at their foreign exchange office for Bulgarian leva, they had given me too much money. They had mistakenly changed my dollars at the higher rate used for Soviet citizens rather than the designated rate for Westerners. Feeling this was their problem rather than mine, I had no intention of driving all the way back to that city for the matter of a few Bulgarian leva.

We worried until we were safely out of Bulgaria that our names had been called ahead to the guards at all borders to not allow us to leave until we returned to the hotel and paid back the extra money. Fortunately, that did not happen.

As I replay that story in mind, the thing that amazes me most is "How in the world did the hotel know where I was?" We had driven for hours to that small, remote village to visit the nondescript apartment of an old, seemingly insignificant woman. Who had been tracking us, and how? The resources used in communist countries to track suspicious persons, like me, seemed unlimited. We never found out who followed us and how they knew that lady's telephone number. Spooky!

After we left the old woman's apartment that Saturday, we needed to drive many hours west through Bulgaria in order to be in Yugoslavia for church on Sunday. The Bulgarian language uses the same Cyrillic script that Russian does, so it was a struggle to read the road signs. However, I had prepared a homemade list of the Cyrillic letters and their English counterparts. For example, the letter that looks like H in Cyrillic is N in English. Whenever we saw the rare road sign, we parked our car and translated the words letter by letter. We then realized, "Oh, we are on the road to Michaelevgrad," or "Here we can go south to Sofia [the capital of Bulgaria]." In Cyrillic letters Sofia, Bulgaria, is София България. Despite being painfully slow, this letter-by-letter translation process proved to be our only solution for navigating Bulgaria.

Upon our arrival at the northernmost border crossing in Yugoslavia, soldiers stationed there barked at us, "This border crossing is closed. No entrance to Yugoslavia! Forbidden!"

"Well, then, how do we get into Yugoslavia?"

"You must go south to the next crossing."

But that crossing was several hundred kilometers to the south. And, because once we were in Yugoslavia we needed to go further north, a detour to the south would cost us many precious hours.

Our hearts sank in dismay and discouragement. Was there no other alternative?

At that point Bill looked at the map and noticed we could drive back east a ways, cross the Danube River, and reenter Romania. Driving north and west through Romania only a short distance, we would find a border crossing into Yugoslavia.

Only one problem: our single-entry visas for Romania had already been used up when we entered Romania from Hungary! But the alternative route Bill discovered would save so much time that we decided to risk it and prayed for success and compassionate hearts at the Romanian border.

Driving back east to the Danube River, we again navigated with the same agonizingly slow process of translating road signs letter by letter. Eventually we happened upon a sign with several destinations written in Cyrillic, but curiously one destination was written in Latin letters, Feribot. We wondered about this Feribot town and searched for it on the map. Suddenly we realized Feribot meant "ferry boat," and were elated. This being exactly what we were looking for, we wondered if an angel had gone ahead of us and painted this essential information on the sign for us.

At the Danube we paid our fee and drove onto the ferry boat. After the boat was full we crossed to the other side of the river and were one of the first cars off. However, the officials shunted us to the side while they processed all the other cars, trucks, motorcycles, and foot passengers. When they finished everyone else, they came back to us.

The border crossing chief saw we didn't have valid visas for reentering Romania and initially turned away from assisting us. Again our hearts sank. Agitated, after a moment or two he turned back to us and shouted, "Tre, tre, tre!" holding up three fingers.

Recalling that we had to pay ten U.S. dollars per person per night of intended stay in Romania, we finally figured out what he meant. Even though we planned to drive for only a couple of hours in Romania, we needed to pay as if we were staying three days. Four people times three days times ten dollars meant $120. It was worth it to us, and we agreed to pay that amount for our Romanian entry visas.

After we paid, the border guards still needed to check our car. They opened all the doors, the hood, and the trunk and set all our stuff on the ground. All suitcases and purses were opened and inspected. Dogs romped through our car, sniffing everything. The guards used mirrors to examine underneath the car.

In both Romania and Bulgaria, we were not allowed to take any of their currency out of the country. It had to be either spent or given back. The Baumgartners had used some of their leftover Bulgarian leva to buy a large urn. We wrapped the urn in a blanket to protect it from breaking. When I saw one of the dogs about to pee on the blanket-covered urn sitting on the ground, I thought that was the final indignity and shouted at it. With that shout I suddenly found a couple of AK-47s aimed at me. I didn't even want to think, though, about the smell we would have endured in our car if that blanket had been soaked by dog urine. The soldiers did chase the dog away from the urn after they saw the reason for my shout.

Finally, after all the bureaucracy, the guards allowed us to pass. Our plans worked out as we had hoped, and we crossed somewhat effortlessly from Romania into Yugoslavia.

Yugoslavia did not seem nearly as oppressive as the other communist countries we visited (excluding Hungary). Without much bureaucracy or hindrance we traveled fairly freely where we wanted and visited the people and churches we wanted to visit. We felt we were on the uphill climb out of the pits of oppression and repression of socialist countries.

As we turned our hearts back toward the West, we traveled up the Yugoslav coast along the beautiful Adriatic Sea, sparking in Peggy an as-yet-unfulfilled desire to take a cruise among the Greek islands. We crossed Italy, put our car on a train to travel through a tunnel into Switzerland, and drove on to Germany to fly back to America and all its blessings.

Including the details of this European trip in a book about my missionary journey may seem like somewhat of a detour. But this trip proved to be a stepping stone rather than a detour. On this very rigorous and exhausting trip we learned a lot about world missions.

World missions isn't just about planting churches, building schools, and starting feeding programs in impoverished countries. God clearly states over and over in His Word that the gospel is about relationships. In Matthew 22:39 (NIV) Jesus stated that the second part of the "greatest commandment" is: "Love your neighbor as yourself." And in the parable of The Good Samaritan He described anyone who crosses our path as a neighbor (Luke 10:25-37).

I regard this trip as a missionary journey entitled "Loving Our Neighbors." Even though it started out as a challenge to see if both of us couples truly were committed to visiting our denomination's churches behind the iron curtain, it became much more than that. Without exception, the church members we met in Eastern Europe could not adequately express how much it meant to have Americans come and visit them. The highest ranking leaders of the churches met with us and confided in us their concerns and aspirations, although we weren't worthy of that.

We saw firsthand the impact of the gospel on people's lives. We saw how tenaciously people cling to the hope of salvation and a home in heaven free from the persecution and oppression that man can impose upon them here on this earth. We saw the extreme measures they took to smuggle Bibles into a land where the Word of God was not available. We saw a few pages of Scripture being passed around from person to person as if they were more precious than gold. And, in reality, they are.

We witnessed firsthand Christians risking imprisonment and torture for possession of the Word of God and for the opportunity for sweet brotherly fellowship with other believers. It seemed nearly everyone had been in prison themselves for their faith or had a close family member who had been in jail.

After returning to the U.S. we realized that for us Eastern Europe was the "uttermost part of the earth" as Jesus said, "Ye shall be witnesses unto me both in Jerusalem, and in all Judaea, and in Samaria, and unto the uttermost part of the earth" (Acts 1:8 KJV). After that experience Peggy and I knew that someday we would return to the uttermost part of the earth and we could never really be content living in "Jerusalem."

CHAPTER 6

Wycliffe Bible Translators Idyllwild, California

Because of the interest in world missions growing inside Peggy and me, we signed our family up for a unique missions experience in 1989. Wycliffe Bible Translators was offering its Quest program (used to acquaint potential missionaries with overseas missions, Wycliffe style) at several locations that year. Our family enrolled in the program at Tahquitz Pines Camp in Idyllwild, California.

Despite the considerable expense of getting the five of us to California, we weighed all the factors and decided to go for it. Our primary purpose for attending Quest was to do something with our children to give them a solid introduction to overseas missions. There were special activities for each age group, including our one-and-a-half-year-old son, Sam.

It sounded like the ideal arrangement. Our kids would enjoy a good summer experience as well as learning about the millions of people who did not yet have any part of the Bible in their "heart language." We hoped they would understand, then, our interest in going overseas as a family and helping to bring God's Word to those millions.

What we did not know was Quest's objective of being a "make it or break it" testing ground for people applying to serve as Wycliffe missionaries. Somehow, this concept never came up when we talked to the Wycliffe staff about our attendance at Quest.

Young, middle-aged, and older people attended to prove to the Wycliffe organization they had what it took to make it in the jungle, the desert, the frozen north, or wherever they might be sent.

With great anticipation we flew to Los Angeles, where a Wycliffe missionary met us to drive us across the desert to the Santa Barbara mountains and the Tahquitz Pines Camp, our home for the next month. The full-sized van we rode in had no windows that opened except those for the front seats. To make our misery complete, the air conditioner was broken, leaving nothing to cool our bodies in the hot June California sun except our own sweat. Oh, our entire family will never forget how hot that trip was! That must have been our first test. We passed, though barely.

When we got to Tahquitz Pines and completed the orientation, we began to understand what we had gotten ourselves into. We had placed our family on a microscope slide to be scrutinized for the next month. During that month, Peggy and I sat through classes all day long, lugging home loads of homework at night.

Our family of five found ourselves cramped into a tiny apartment. Since Peggy and I had so much work to do in the evening and needed to study for tests, we put up a blanket in front of Sam's bed, hoping he would go to sleep early. However, he didn't understand our predicament and wanted to be in on the action. The poor little boy peeked around his curtain, crying for attention and to be taken from his crib. His plaintive cries raised the stress level of our family; we all became edgy and grated on each other's nerves.

In addition to the academics (including learning Papua New Guinea's pidgin language), our instructors gave us batteries of psychological tests, skills tests (such as Meyers-Briggs), Bible tests, emotional tests, and physical tests. If that weren't enough, we had to take our turns with the meals, setting up the tables, washing dishes, cleaning up, and helping with food preparation.

We hadn't enrolled in Quest with the intention of moving forward with our Wycliffe membership. We only intended it to be a fun educational experience to acquaint our children with missionary life. We didn't expect army boot camp.

One young couple, both children of Wycliffe missionaries in Brazil, attended with their three children. This family desperately needed to pass Quest to achieve their objective of becoming full-time Wycliffe missionaries in Brazil. Toward the end of the month of Quest, the husband was admitted to the hospital with panic attacks. Other people also came down with illnesses and had to drop out.

Some found out they needed to go to Bible college to improve their familiarity with the Scriptures. Others were told they needed to go to school for linguistics or English, or needed to lose weight, or any number of things. Our family plowed on, passing our tests and avoiding additional assignments.

In our final evaluation we learned that both Peggy and I had passed everything. No need for Bible college (our test scores on familiarity with Scriptures were higher than some Bible college graduates'), no need for more schooling; we were qualified to begin the process of becoming full-fledged Wycliffe members immediately. And we hadn't even enrolled in Quest with that intention! We felt very encouraged by these results, but it left us in a quandary as to how to proceed.

This unexpected success made Peggy and me wonder if God had ordained this time for us to become full-time missionaries. "If we are so well prepared, should we forge ahead?" we asked ourselves.

The dream of being a Bible translator was what had originally attracted me to Wycliffe. I dreamed of being the man who brought the Bible to some remote people group who had never heard (nor read) the Word of God in their heart language.

But as we discussed the process of moving forward as missionaries with the Wycliffe personnel, I learned they had other ideas. Because of my MBA and years of management experience at State Farm Insurance, they wanted me to be an administrator. They told me that finding good administrators within the Wycliffe organization proved harder than finding good translators. They always felt guilty taking a translator off his or her translation project to bring him or her into the branch office to take over administrative responsibilities.

We later learned this truth firsthand. Due to the desperate need for management staff, a translation project often was put on hold to allow the translator to become an administrator. And, unfortunately, as we also found out later, translators often don't make the best administrators.

In addition to that new information, our counselors told me my age prevented my becoming a translator. Translators, according to them, needed to be age thirty-four or younger, and I missed this cutoff by six years. They had determined that after age thirty-four, the rigors of a remote translator's life were too tough. In addition, since it usually takes fifteen to twenty years to translate the New Testament, by the time the translation is completed the missionary is quite old and may have lost his effectiveness. I strongly disagreed with that argument, but I relented and told them I would consider the administrative track.

When Peggy and I dug deeper into the process of going forward, we started to think practically about how these changes would impact our family. Completing intercultural training in a foreign country would be our first assignment. Following cultural training, we would go to school for our specialty—in my case it was administration. After that specialized training we would probably go to Mexico, Cameroon, Kenya, or the Philippines for "jungle camp." When we completed jungle camp we would likely go to another country for language training.

If West Africa, for example, were to be our final destination, we would study French in France or Switzerland, since West Africa is a francophone area. Following language training would be an internship in a country other than our final assignment. Surprisingly, they told us we needed to complete the internship because they believed our mistakes should be made under the supervision of someone else, before we embarked upon that kind of work on our own.

For our daughters, ages thirteen and ten (eighth grade and fifth grade), the thought of all that moving—likely to be five countries in the next five years—overwhelmed them. They dug in their heels and protested.

Peggy and I thought that if God was calling us to the mission field, we should be obedient and go. But we didn't want to go at the expense of tearing apart our family.

We were in a quandary.

In desperation we made appointments with executives of SIL in Dallas, Texas. SIL used to stand for Summer Institute of Linguistics, a summer training course for Wycliffe linguists. That long name was changed to simply SIL and is how Wycliffe is now known overseas. SIL and Wycliffe Bible Translators are sister organizations with separate bylaws and boards of directors.

We flew to Dallas and explained our situation. Since we had passed Quest and all our other tests and were approved as Wycliffe MITs (Members in Training), we told those officials of our desire to proceed. We also informed them of our daughters' reluctance to commit to all the potential travel and disruption of their lives over the next few years.

The SIL officials stuck to their guns and explained that even though they understood our plight, the protocol was not flexible. We boarded the airplane back to Illinois with our tails tucked between our legs.

Following that disappointing experience, I wrote a letter to the president of Wycliffe Bible Translators, Bernie May, pleading our case to him. Bernie wrote back, also stating that he understood our situation and empathized with us, but even he couldn't make any exceptions.

In near desperation, I learned of another person I could contact. I found out the regional vice-president (the highest ranking officer) of the Southern California regional office of State Farm, Roger Tompkins, was on the board of directors of Wycliffe. I wrote a letter to him, explaining our dual connection of Wycliffe and State Farm and asking if he could intercede for me.

Roger wrote back that he was going to State Farm corporate headquarters soon and would look me up so we could talk face to face. True to his word he came to my office, and I felt humbled to have a State Farm VP visiting me. We discussed the situation, and he had a prayer with me. Roger replied there was really nothing he could do to fast-track us to the field without going through the intermediary steps.

Because of these obstacles, we eventually let our Member in Training status lapse. God, without divulging the details, seemed to be telling us that there was something in store for us...just not yet. He had nailed the Wycliffe door firmly shut for the time being.

CHAPTER 7

Wycliffe Associates England

Have you ever thought about celebrating American Independence Day—the Fourth of July—in, of all places, England? We hadn't thought about it either until we actually did that on a short-term mission trip to England with Wycliffe Associates in July 1993.

In early 1993 we began looking for another unique overseas mission experience to share with our children. We wanted something that would be a meaningful family vacation but also instructive and informative for the kids to learn more about overseas missions. However, we didn't want another boot camp, like Quest had been four years before.

So, what better way to accomplish that than go overseas and do actual mission work? When we went to Brazil in 1982, our daughters were too young to understand that experience. Our summer with Wycliffe Bible Translators at Tahquitz Pines, California, was all about foreign missions but was not "foreign" and not actually "doing missions."

In spite of our disappointment with how our discussions with SIL officials regarding a full-time overseas mission assignment had turned out four years prior, our admiration for the work of Wycliffe did not waver. We were excited to find a short-term opportunity with Wycliffe Associates in England that fit our schedule and met our desires. The project involved my helping build a childcare center on the Horsley's Green campus of Wycliffe Bible Translators in England, located midway between London and Oxford.

I know, I know, modern and highly economically developed England isn't the first place that comes to mind when thinking about foreign missions or typical missionary work. But the work needed to be done to further the spread of the gospel. Our family voted unanimously to go.

We stayed in the smallest of all possible apartments. In Peggy's and my bedroom there was just enough room to walk around the bed; I could not even kneel beside the bed to pray. The kids shared another tiny room adjacent to ours. They slept on mattresses on the floor. We all had to use a common toilet and shower down the hall. Fortunately, everyone was a good sport about this difficult situation.

I joined a small team consisting of one other Wycliffe Associates volunteer, Richard from California, and a few young volunteers, who were called "vollies," from England and other European countries.

Each morning we construction workers began with a short devotion and then started work. I spent my days either muscling around wheelbarrows full of concrete or up on the roof of the childcare center (or should I say centre?). Being a sedentary State Farm office employee, this physical work really taxed my muscles, and I returned to our apartment each evening dirtier than at any time since my days as a farm boy. Knowing that I would soon return to a job with physical activity limited to hiking in from the parking lot and that many children would spend happy days in this childcare center, I had no problem arising each morning to face the task.

Peggy and Angie never knew what their day's work would entail. Some days they prepared food, some days they ironed, and others they sewed curtains. Due to very strict child labor laws in Great Britain, Becky (at age thirteen) could do nothing resembling work for pay. However, she did a great job of caring for Sam (age five) every day while the rest of us went about our tasks. The few British pounds we gave Becky each morning to buy candy and ice cream for herself and Sam at the "sweet shop" across the street gave them something to look forward to.

British building construction is quite different from American construction. For some reason, when they finish the walls there is a gap between the top of the wall and the ceiling. This gap must be caulked. My soft muscles groaned as I tried to do an accurate and neat job while standing on a ladder, holding my arms above my head all day.

At one point, Peggy came to visit me while I stood on the ladder caulking the crack. "What are you doing?" she asked.

"I'm helping to get Bibles translated in Africa," I replied, displaying my caulking gun and thinking it should be fairly obvious what I was doing.

That statement technically was true, as the Wycliffe office at Horsley's Green oversaw work in Africa. But little did I know how it would literally be fulfilled less than eight years later.

We couldn't have picked a more appropriate country to visit at that point in Sam's life. He idolized Robin Hood and saw a weapon in every stick he held. He had three friends his age at the Wycliffe compound, and they played hard together every day. One friend was English, another Korean, and the third a Spanish-speaking Peruvian. Day after day they ran over and around the construction dirt piles, cement blocks, and other building materials with sticks as guns and bows and arrows, playing "Robin Hood."

I found their playing together in three different languages fascinating. So I asked Sam how they could play together when they couldn't even speak each other's languages. He looked at me with the most unbelievable expression, not having any idea what I was talking about. They were playing and thus "communicating"—no problem, don't worry, Dad! Another lesson in linguistics for me: children don't communicate the same way adults do. And they don't hesitate, like adults do, to try to communicate with people who speak other languages. We can learn a lot from that.

On the weekends our family enjoyed visiting various parts of Great Britain. The first weekend Angie and I took the bus to Oxford, found the Hertz car rental office, and rented a car. I had never driven on the left side of the road before. So as I drove out of the car rental lot I kept telling myself I was sitting on the right side of the car and needed to drive on the left side of the road. I was especially dreading a huge roundabout that I knew I needed to traverse immediately after leaving the rental car lot. As I was driving through the parking lot on my way to the street, I saw a car coming directly at me. I stopped, temporarily confused. Angie looked over at me and said, "Dad, I think you need to start driving on the left side even before you get to the street."

The first weekend we traveled west all the way to the Devon peninsula, stopping along the way to visit Stonehenge and other attractions. We returned to the Wycliffe compound on the Fourth of July. We found that the few other Americans had taken their celebration down to the far end of the meadow to have a large meal and play with sparklers without rubbing it in the faces of our British friends. It felt a little eerie to celebrate this important American holiday in England, even though the American Revolution took place 217 years before.

By the second weekend I felt comfortable driving on the left side of the road. We drove north up to Manchester and back down through Wales. The thing I remember about Wales is that the Welsh language doesn't at all resemble English. They lack a lot of vowels. As a matter of fact, they are so desperate for vowels they regularly use w and y in their place. They should borrow some vowels from Dutch or Oromo (in Ethiopia), as those languages have an excess of vowels. For example, Welsh for "hello" is shwmae (sho-MY-ee) and for "Wales" Cymru (KOOM-ree).

On this northern trip I did something I still feel bad about to this day. When we saw signs for Nottingham, Sam was sound asleep in the back seat. As we passed the entrance to Sherwood Forest and a statue of Robin Hood, I motioned for the family to be very quiet, or otherwise the rest of the day would be spent watching Sam explore Sherwood Forest, looking for King Arthur and his Knights of the Round Table. Sam has gotten over it, but I still feel a little bad about it.

Three weeks in England wouldn't be complete without exploring London. Driving ourselves would have been disastrous in that big, bustling city, so we took advantage of the excellent public transportation, including buses and the "Tube" (Metro). We took the obligatory double-decker red bus tour, visited the Tower of London and Westminster Abbey, and saw the River Thames, Buckingham Palace, Big Ben, Parliament, and all the other touristy sites.

None of us will ever forget that trip.

We learned to appreciate and understand the work of Wycliffe Bible Translators around the world while meeting many wonderful and dedicated people. A lot of scholarly activity took place on that campus, and the missionaries worked diligently to move the work of Bible translation steadily forward.

As a matter of fact, some of the people we interacted with intimidated me with their scholarliness. Many had earned PhDs, and their credentials allowed them to list lots of other letters after their names. One day in chapel I explained what our family had come to England to do. After hearing my story one person commented, "What a good example of practical Christianity!" I was somewhat taken aback by that statement, because in my mind Christianity should be practical and something the common person can relate to.

As the weeks passed I saw more clearly the need for both practical and theoretical work on the mission field. In the end I felt a balance between the two was best. While I felt intimidated by some of their scholarly dissertations, their numbers of books published, and their high-falutin' speech, I also felt sorry for someone who didn't have a clue as to how to change oil in his car or wire a simple electrical switch.

Fortunately, God is in control and gives each of us unique talents. What He desires is for us to use those gifts for His work and not waste our precious talents.

CHAPTER 8

Jamaica

In 1995 our local Bloomington church did something revolutionary for the entire denomination. Several of us members discussed the possibility of sending the high-school-aged members of our Sunday school (also known as the Bible class) on an overseas missions trip. Given the stance of our denomination toward missions at the time, taking our young people on a foreign missions trip was a radical concept. However, this idea grew in popularity throughout our local congregation, and our church leaders encouraged us to form a committee to explore the possibilities.

As with introducing any sweeping change into a society, we believed that if you can convert and change the young people, eventually the idea will take hold in the society as a whole. For those of us who are members of the Apostolic Christian Church, a significant part of our identity is found in our church affiliation, our "society."

From 1986 to 1993 I represented the eastern half of Illinois on the Apostolic Christian Church National World Relief Committee. During this time I became very familiar with the overseas relief and development work our denomination supported. However, "spiritual" projects such as planting churches or evangelizing still were not "sanctioned."

Given my familiarity with overseas work projects, the newly formed committee asked me to explore the possible projects for a foreign missions trip for the young people.

Jamaica had recently opened up as an alternative to Haiti for foreign relief work. We had begun supporting a mission in Jamaica called CCCD (Caribbean Christian Centre for the Deaf). After examining my list of the various projects available in Haiti and Jamaica, the committee decided to pursue a project with CCCD. They could handle the logistics of a large team while providing opportunities for people with a variety of skills.

In order to make this trip a reality, we needed to sell the concept to the Bloomington church as a whole. We presented our proposal to the church leadership, and they unanimously approved. Everett Hari, our newly appointed elder, backed us completely. (On a personal note, Everett supported Peggy and me in our missionary endeavors so solidly that we could never thank him enough. We will never know all the barriers he knocked down for us nor the criticism he undoubtedly received on our behalf. He was truly a missions pioneer for the Apostolic Christian Church.)

Our committee didn't want to make participation in the trip a financial burden on any student or family. We wanted all Bible class students to go, regardless of their financial situation. We asked each team member to contribute $100, and the rest came in through fund-raising activities.

In the meantime our subcommittees worked with CCCD to determine what types of activities our team could participate in while in Jamaica. CCCD had established three different sites on the island, each with its unique activities. After reviewing all the information and the pros and cons, our committee decided to focus on the campus in Kingston. There would be construction work (raising the wall around the compound, pouring a concrete driveway, destruction of one building to rebuild a larger one, etc.),

Vacation Bible School, gardening (tree and bush planting), and other activities involving the children of the campus.

All children at CCCD are deaf, so the education they receive prepares them to face life—a life of no voice conversations, music, or enjoyment of simply listening to birds, teachers, crickets chirping, or thunder. But through sign language the children are given the ability to function as productive citizens of society.

As an example of the challenges these deaf children face, one day I saw one of the CCCD girls about to walk through wet cement. Instinctively I yelled for her to watch out, but she heard nothing and walked right into the previously poured and troweled concrete. For a hearing child this problem would have been easily avoided. But this girl had to endure cement-coated shoes and socks and the embarrassment of having messed up someone's hard work.

Without many problems we raised the funds and finalized the preparations. On the long-anticipated day of departure we traveled by bus to Chicago O'Hare for our flight to Miami and on to Kingston, Jamaica.

Ron Hodel and his wife, Donna, have been close friends of ours for many years. We both worked at State Farm and attended the same church. He was a true businessman, and if anything within our local church needed to be organized or administered, we often called on Ron to do it.

Ron had been on a previous mission trip to the island of St. Vincent with me and had gotten infected by the missions "bug." That experience made him a willing volunteer for future missions trips. Over the years he has served in a number of capacities within the local church, and for the denomination as a whole, on mission committees. So Ron naturally emerged as co-leader of the Jamaica team and the right man for the job to keep everything in order and on schedule. He helped us organize the students and adults into OAs and YAs.

Beginning with boarding the bus to O'Hare from our church parking lot, each OA (Older Adult) was responsible for two or three YAs (Young Adults). This task required keeping close tabs on the YAs at all times, passing along announcements and instructions to them, and making sure they stayed gainfully occupied. This system worked very well, and the friendships forged between some OAs and YAs remain strong today.

My main responsibility, other than leadership activities, was forming and pouring concrete for the driveway, particularly the ramp from the gate up to the main driveway level of the compound. I was surprised when our daughter Becky, a student on the trip, chose to volunteer for my project. Even though she had previously voiced her concern about her parents cramping her style around her friends, she chose to be on my team, which made me proud and happy. She had the opportunity to volunteer for jobs that didn't require so much physical labor but chose one that involved very hard labor (and her dad). Bless her!

This missions trip to Jamaica blessed everyone who participated. The teachers and students, adults and teenagers all got to know each other very well. And getting to know and understand each other well is basic to good communication, especially across generations.

The teenagers on the team stuck out as being especially passionate and solid in their love for Jesus and their desire to follow Him. Becky and almost all of her Sunday school classmates became Christians while still in high school. And they have grown and prospered in their Christian walk. Many are serving the church or the community in ways that are Spirit-directed.

In addition, many from that group still demonstrate a strong interest in world missions. Some of these young people have gone overseas on other short-term trips. Others have found Christ-centered ministerial or occupational positions domestically within the U.S.

After the Bloomington experience, other local churches started to also send their Sunday school classes on overseas missions trips. The concept of high schoolers traveling overseas to serve has snowballed, and now there is nothing unique or extraordinary about hearing of a group of teenagers from the Apostolic Christian Church volunteering for mission activities all around the world.

This experience really did revolutionize the entire denomination. There has been a huge positive change of attitude and support with regard to missions and missionaries. God wants the good news about His Son spread to the far corners of the world. Often He calls on His people to step out in faith and try new methods to achieve His purpose. Sending young people out of their comfort zones was one of those new methods.

CHAPTER 9

Brazil, Again!

After living in the Amazon basin for several years, my cousin Luke Huber taught himself to fly an ultralight airplane. An ultralight is not much more than a wing and a small motor with a place for the pilot to strap himself in. For Luke, flying from one PAZ base to another or to the widely scattered churches in his ultralight opened doors previously closed to his ministry. With his little airplane he could reach distant villages in hours compared with the days a riverboat would take to travel the same distance.

Tragically, in 1994, as Luke took off in his ultralight to return to PAZ headquarters from a far-flung location, the plane mysteriously stalled out and crashed into the Amazon River, killing Luke and injuring a fellow passenger. Luke died as he probably would have wished to have died. Spreading God's Word to the people of the Amazon River basin was his life's work and source of his fulfillment and feeling of accomplishment. The little airplane was his tool to help him do that more effectively.

Luke's untimely and premature death thrust the responsibility and accompanying burden of running Project AmaZon onto his younger sister, Becky, and her husband, Jeff Hrubik.

Our kids had grown up hearing about their cousins in Brazil but hardly remembered them or our previous trip to Brazil, which had taken place five years before Sam was born. So, Peggy and I decided to take another trip to let our children experience Brazil at a time they would remember. Because I had carried over my vacation at State Farm from the previous year, we were able to plan to stay for a month.

Once again, our family flew off together to another mission experience. And, once again, the oppressive Brazilian heat greeted us, and we sweated just as freely as we had sixteen years before. But all the changes and advancements that had taken place over the intervening years impressed us more than the stifling heat. Since our first trip to Brazil, the following had occurred:

> Melvin and Katherine, and their oldest daughter, Angela, had moved far upstream to an island in the middle of the Amazon River called Parintins. They focused on evangelizing and planting a church on that large island.
>
> Another cousin of mine, Scott Blunier, and his wife, Aldine, and their three daughters lived there. Scott is the accountant for PAZ.
>
> The PAZ Central Church, which was just getting its feet on the ground back in 1982, had become a huge edifice with four or five services every weekend. My youngest Huber cousin, Abe, pastored that church.
>
> A number of other PAZ churches had been started in Santarém and were thriving. These were in addition to the hundreds of other churches the mission had established in the outlying regions.
>
> Many other missionaries from various backgrounds also served there.
>
> The homes and offices of the PAZ missionaries were nicer and larger, and some even had air conditioning.
>
> In contrast to the small "seat of the pants" operation we found in 1982, PAZ operated as an organization firmly established, computerized, with television and radio pro-

grams and all other kinds of media outreaches, both in Brazil and overseas.

Project AmaZon and its missionaries had a solid, well-respected presence in that area of Brazil, recognized by the local and state governments.

Our family settled in at the comfortable guest house and soon began to figure out our roles for the month. Sam, at age ten, quickly discovered fun in the jungle. His young buddies showed him the availability of firecrackers at seemingly every local shop, and soon they were blowing up everything within blocks. Although we feared all the noise would attract the attention of the police, I don't believe that ever happened. Waking up napping missionary kids was, to my knowledge, the worst crime they perpetrated.

During the month we traveled by overnight commercial lineboat to the island of Parintins, where Melvin, Katherine, and Angela lived. For our sleeping accommodations we hung our hammocks within the maze of our fellow travelers' hammocks and rocked in our cloth cradles until we got to Parintins. A wind came up during the night and blew Angie's hammock back and forth out over the river in the midst of the spray from the boat. It was an exciting (translated as frightening) ride for her.

Our family helped the Hubers with several different projects at Parintins. I helped Uncle Melvin build cabinetry and shelves in a church they were remodeling, utilizing my woodworking skills I had developed in our basement over the years. Other days we spent our time building and painting an open-sided meeting hall on property the Hubers had acquired. They intended to convert the property into a place to train pastors and evangelists, while also providing opportunities for relaxation and Bible studies.

Melvin and Katherine had named their two daughters Angela and Rebecca, the same as our two daughters. This may be confusing, but each set of "Angela and Rebecca" is from a different generation. Although we didn't name our daughters after their daughters, I'm sure they wouldn't have minded if we had. When our first daughter was born we wanted her to be called Angie, so we named her Angela. We named our Rebecca after a foster daughter, Becky, whom we had taken into our home for several months. After the foster daughter left our family and our second daughter was born, we couldn't imagine being without a Becky of our very own.

One day Angela Huber offered to take Peggy and me to a remote Amazon village to visit an Indian tribe she was evangelizing. Brazilian federal and state law forbids outsiders from interacting with indigenous tribes, to prevent them from being spoiled by modern ideas and technology.

At that time, I didn't have a strong opinion about laws forbidding interaction between indigenous "stone age" tribes and the developed world. But after years of working in Africa, I now strongly disagree with that kind of regulation. It may sound exotic to leave a tribe unspoiled by the influence of modern man. However, the idea of a native "savage" living a blissful, innocent lifestyle is only a pipe dream meant to salve the consciences of the First World.

Which people group wouldn't want the benefits of modern medicine for broken bones or malaria or meningitis or difficult childbirth? Why wouldn't they want to be educated—to learn how to farm better or to build better homes or eat better food? Who wouldn't want to satisfy their curiosity, to develop and explore like man has done since the beginning of time? And, most importantly (although, unfortunately, many non-Christians do not agree with this) these people also deserve to hear about Jesus Christ and the plan for man's salvation that He sacrificed His life for.

Even though Angela could not legally step onto their land, she occasionally traveled to this tribe's village by boat and stopped out in the middle of the river. When her Indian friends spied her, tribe members eagerly rowed out to visit with her. Since the river was "public" she could legally witness to them in this manner.

Peggy and I enthusiastically accepted Angela's invitation. We, along with the driver, traveled by speedboat up one tributary of the Amazon to a tributary of that tributary to the village. As anticipated, when Angela's friends saw us coming, they rowed out to meet us. We talked for a while out in the middle of the river current. Eventually they invited us to come on shore with them. Honoring the law forbidding such activity, we hesitated; however, they insisted. So we followed them to the river bank and stepped onto forbidden land.

They were eager to show us all the activities of their village. We saw one large group working together making farinha, a tapioca-like food made from the root of the cassava plant. But a most remarkable incident occurred when they called three girls to come sing for us. The girls sang beautifully, and we complimented them profusely.

During the performance, I spied one young man slipping away from the group. A few minutes later he returned with, of all things, a portable tape recorder that used batteries. So much for keeping these "primitive savages" from modern influence! I wondered how the batteries could still be good out there in the middle of nowhere with the humid jungle climate. But the man turned the tape recorder on, and we again heard the voices of those three girls, singing different songs. The drive of man to better himself and to enjoy the advances of technology is very powerful!

On the island of Parintins the battle with the evil spirit world raged openly. We arrived just before the start of the Festival of the Bull, an occasion similar to the lewd and lascivious celebration of Carnaval in other parts of Brazil. For months leading up to the actual festival each year, two teams spend thousands of hours preparing parade floats and huge remote-controlled, animated, evil-looking and demonic mechanized characters to be revealed on the day of the festival. The technology, electronics, and computer controls that went into making these "walking," fire-breathing, bellowing animal and demon representations boggled my mind. Horns, evil eyes, scales, and every imaginable satanic depiction made the floats look as scary and fiendish as possible. And some of them were fifty to sixty feet (fifteen to twenty meters) long, towering two to three stories high.

Even though entry to the assembly buildings for these creatures normally was forbidden to all outsiders, Angela, through her connections, obtained permission for us to visit one of them. The creators showed us the amazing devices in all stages of preparation and explained how they controlled them, how they could make their eyes seem to glow, how the devices moved, and how they appeared to breathe fire from their nostrils.

During the festival they intended to take these beasts to the soccer stadium and introduce them to the roaring masses of revelers. Every evil vice, including drinking, drugs, and lewdness, would be present, and these figures were the culmination of the celebration. Judges chose a winning team, and that team earned honor and recognition for the coming year.

The activities surrounding the Festival of the Bull diametrically opposed all Christian values and greatly troubled the small group of believers on the island. The people of Parintins needed to hear the good news of Jesus Christ rather than the lies of Satan. So during our visit, our small group marched daily around the soccer stadium where the festival was scheduled to be held, praying against the evil forces of Satan and his demons. We walked, Bibles in hand, praying for a release of the island from the clutches of the evil spirits.

The spiritual oppression on Parintins Island was palpable, especially as the day of the judging of the teams' creations approached. Our itinerary called us back to Santarém before the actual day of the Festival of the Bull. We left Parintins desiring closure to our activities and wondering how the festival would turn out.

After a month filled with new experiences and rewarding activities, we returned to the States. On the airplane back to Miami, our Becky sat just a few rows behind me and carried on a lively conversation with the young man sitting beside her. I couldn't hear the conversation, but I could tell the subject was quite intense.

When we landed in Miami I couldn't wait to find out what they had talked about. Becky excitedly explained that the man she had been talking to was a technician hired by the Parintins team whose building we had visited. He described his experience as so miserable that he would never go back. Rain messed up most of the program where they planned to display their evil-looking beasts. When they took their biggest and proudest creation out of the building and sent it upon its way to the stadium, it abruptly short-circuited, and the giant contraption collapsed into a worthless pile of scrap metal! He told Becky that the large number of problems made him suspect there was some force opposing them.

There was. And we were quite aware of who He is.

I have rarely been involved in such an obvious manifestation of answer to prayer. To hear about such a dramatic display of God's direct response to our earnest pleas was a real faith-builder. This incident, along with others we experienced during our month in Brazil, reinforced our understanding that this trip was focused more on the spiritual realm, the battle between the forces of good and evil.

One of the changes we noticed in comparing this trip to our trip sixteen years prior was a greater emphasis on the utilization of the charismatic gifts of the spirit by the PAZ church. Peggy and I know these gifts are documented in the Bible. We also know the Holy Spirit lives among believers and constantly works within them. As believers exercise their spiritual gifts, God and His kingdom are glorified. We have nothing whatsoever against the charismatic gifts; nor do we in any way deny them and their effectiveness. As long as they are used according to scriptural guidelines without guile or deceit and not to give glory or honor to any human being, they are powerful tools.

Our experiences in Brazil proved very useful to us two years later when we were making our decision as to which foreign mission organization to join. We, of course, love our "Brazilian" relatives and place them on a pedestal for the examples they have been to us and for their sacrificial lives. I have dedicated this book to them. Whenever we have a chance to meet with any of them in the U.S. we eagerly anticipate seeing them. But when we faced the decision of whether to join PAZ or not, having been accustomed to our lifelong conservative Christian background, the idea of working in that charismatic setting did not give us peace in our hearts that that was where God wanted us to serve.

CHAPTER 10

Be Patient!

God continued to fan the flames of missionary service within our hearts over the years by opening up additional opportunities for us in addition to the trips described in the previous chapters. However, He also seemed to continue to warn us to "be patient, the time is not yet right." We served Him on several more short-term trips, gaining more experience, learning about additional ways of serving, and meeting new people. "But," we felt His voice within us saying, "It's not yet your turn. Don't run ahead of Me."

Each of the following experiences played a significant role in my missionary journey. However, I will recap them only briefly.

Haiti (Two More Times)

I returned to Haiti on a well-drilling project in the rural village of Cavignon. While there, our team of three men established great friendships with the people and had opportunities to tell many people about the good news of Jesus. The children came day after day to watch the well-drilling rig claw its way into the earth. And during our days in their village, adults stopped by to watch and marvel at our work. Many took the opportunity to thank us. In the end we left them with a well that provided fresh, clean water for their village.

As often as possible, we explained that the purpose of our work was to glorify our Lord Jesus Christ and that He deserved the praise and thanks. Some of the villagers had already received Jesus as their Savior, and we encouraged them to be strong in their faith. To those who did not yet know Jesus, we explained through an interpreter that knowing Jesus Christ is the most important thing in the world. Again I felt very comfortable being overseas in a missionary situation. I eagerly looked forward to the next time.

Next time arrived three years later. I organized a team from our Bloomington church to visit the farthest point of the southern peninsula of Haiti, a village called Port-a-Piment, with the goal of building a school for the MEBSH (Mission of Evangelical Baptists of South Haiti) Church.

It was the first mission trip for many of the team members, and for some their very first trip overseas. Traveling to Port-a-Piment, so far from anything familiar, in a desperately poverty-stricken country, was considered by some team members as a trip to the edge of the earth. I, on the other hand, felt we could only see the edge from where we were. After fording our vehicles through the fifteenth river on our trek to this desolate town, many of the team members felt we had gone too far.

We stayed at the pastor's house with the throbbing of voodoo drums echoing among the surrounding hills throughout the night. Loud voices cascaded through the town at all hours. Large spiders and rats made their homes in our rooms. We completed the construction of the floor and walls of the school, but not without some rattled psyches.

St. Vincent

The year after my fourth trip to Haiti I led a mission team, in conjunction with Worldteam, to the island of St. Vincent, which is essentially a volcano rising out of the Caribbean Sea. The Vincentians welcomed us warmly and provided wonderful hospitality throughout our stay.

While on St. Vincent we helped to build a church. Each day

we worked with both believers and non-believers and had many interested onlookers. Our work gave us many good opportunities to be a witness for Jesus. Despite the difference in our cultures we quickly felt that common bond with the local believers through the love of Jesus Christ, which transcends all languages, skin colors, and people groups.

Russia

After our trip to Eastern Europe and the Soviet Union, I ached to return to Russia (albeit our previous trip had technically been to the Soviet Republic of Ukraine) to see how things had changed in her transition from a communist to a capitalist society. My opportunity came in 1996.

Headed by Dr. Bruce Wilkinson of Walk Thru the Bible, fifteen mission organizations came together to form the CoMission. Mission organizations and mission leaders that previously had never considered working together joined hand-in-hand to take advantage of the window of opportunity presented in Russia and Romania for teaching Christianity and the Bible in the public schools. The Russian and Romanian governments welcomed Christian teachers to teach their students about the Bible, because the school officials wished to replace the oppressive atheistic school curricula in place since the Bolshevik Revolution of 1917.

Worldteam was one of the CoMission participating missions, and my friend Hod Getz coordinated their work. Worldteam developed a system of rotating missionaries to Russia for one-year terms, with many staying longer. Hod accompanied the new missionaries to Russia, coordinated their orientation, and returned several times a year for training and encouragement.

I found the economic situation in Russia greatly improved from our 1985 visit to Ukraine. Instead of using shabby Soviet-made products, the people took photographs with Japanese cameras, drove Mercedes Benz cars, and used Western appliances in their homes. In addition to the economic changes, I saw none of the severe oppression I observed on my first trip. The citizens interacted more openly with each other, welcomed foreigners, and freely pursued their own interests rather than the state's. I was excited to see open expressions of their newfound freedom of worship.

As for me personally, the trip further confirmed my desire to pursue foreign missions. Observing the CoMission missionaries, ordinary people who had come from all walks of life, working, teaching and evangelizing in a culture very different from their own, reinforced in me the thought that I, too, could do it.

Tobago

By 1999 all of the students from our local church who had participated in the pioneer mission trip to Jamaica had graduated from high school. Our congregation wanted the new Bible class to enjoy the same type of experience.

I was happy to again serve on the committee to oversee the work project part of the trip. Our church leaders voted to take this group of students (and adults, sixty-four people altogether) to Tobago. Tobago is the smaller of the two islands that comprise the nation of Trinidad and Tobago, lying just off the coast of Venezuela. Tobago definitely was not on the list of sanctioned sites for Apostolic Christian overseas work, but the Lord worked it all out regardless.

While in Tobago some team members conducted Vacation Bible School, a construction crew expanded a local church building, and others participated in door-to-door evangelism. The third activity was something that previously had not been a part of the Apostolic Christian Church's missions repertoire.

God provided a blessed and fruitful experience in Tobago. Even though our team seemed to overwhelm the tiny island in everything we did, each team member came away convinced they had experienced a good thing. And another large group of young people's lives changed forever with regard to their understanding of and attitude toward world missions.

As for Peggy and me, the trip added another to the already long list of confirmations of our desire to serve God overseas somewhere. Time was marching on. However, we did not feel Tobago calling us back to full-time service. But that experience fanned the flames of missions even stronger within our hearts. We felt confident that fire would not be extinguished.

CHAPTER 11

God's Call Finally Comes

I knew Scott Shaffer as a State Farm attorney who often reviewed contracts for my staff in the purchasing division, where I worked for many years. When I received an invitation to have coffee with him one evening at a mutual friend's house, I was curious as to what to expect.

Scott, along with a small group of dedicated Christians, was conducting these "coffee meetings" in an attempt to establish a men's Bible Study Fellowship (BSF) group in Bloomington-Normal. The informal gatherings reached out to Christian men, trying to determine the level of interest in having a men's BSF in our community.

Bible Study Fellowship, a very highly structured and intense method of studying the Scriptures, holds its participants accountable to dig into the Bible for themselves. This is not a spoon-fed baby formula program of learning. By focusing each year on a book of the Bible (e.g., Romans) or a Biblical figure's life (e.g., Moses), BSF, at that time, rotated through its curriculum every seven years. "Highly structured" is not an exaggeration. Men and women study in separate BSF classes. Each week, the evening meeting starts exactly on time and the agenda is scheduled to the minute, including wrapping up exactly on time. Discussion of the week's lesson takes thirty-eight minutes; two minutes are allowed for prayer requests.

Such a cold, clinical summarization of BSF may raise the question of whether relationship-building among the participants can actually occur. But it most certainly does occur. By the end of the term of study, the men in each group have bonded and often continue as good friends well into the future. I think that's the reason for the F in BSF.

Scott asked me to be a discussion leader for one of the groups of fifteen men (never more than fifteen; less than fifteen only if there weren't enough men to completely fill a group). The responsibility of leadership required me to complete all the activities of a regular BSF member as well the extra duties assigned to the leaders. We leaders were expected to attend the weekly 6:30 a.m. Saturday leader's meeting. On dark and cold winter mornings it takes a lot of willpower to crawl out of a warm bed on a day off of work to make it to the meeting on time. However, those weekly meetings were often a highlight of my week.

Women's BSF had arrived in Bloomington-Normal several years before, so Peggy had already been serving as an enthusiastic and active participant and leader for some time. In February 2000 (the month of our 25th wedding anniversary), BSF conducted a weekend leaders' retreat near Chicago. Peggy and I drove to the retreat Friday afternoon, and our good friend Dennis Frank rode along.

The BSF executive leaders filled our weekend with excellent, thought-provoking lectures and discussions. On Sunday morning, after Rosemary Jensen, executive director of BSF, gave a lecture, she passed out a questionnaire to all participants. She instructed us to find a quiet place to be alone and fill out the questionnaire. No speaking was allowed, not even with a spouse! We had directions to return to the lecture hall at the appointed time with our completed forms.

Each of the hundreds of participants slipped away to find a quiet place to complete the four-page questionnaire. There were many questions to answer, along with a lot of Bible references for us to look up to help substantiate our answers. But it was the first two questions that had a tremendous impact on Peggy's and my lives.

The first question read something like "If you could do anything that you wanted to do with your life, what would that be?"

The second question followed: "Why aren't you doing it?"

Without hesitation, I answered the first question. "Be a missionary in a foreign country."

The second question I answered, "I don't know."

When Peggy and I finally got back together in our hotel room, we asked each other how we had answered those first two questions. I told Peggy my answers. Following that, she told me she had answered them as follows:

First Question: "Be an overseas missionary."
Second Question: "Because my husband isn't ready."

We looked at each other and then and there decided, "If that's what both of us want to do, then why don't we do it?" That dramatic decision resulted in a monumental life change for me, ranking just a notch below the decision to repent of my sins and give my life to Jesus thirty-two years earlier.

When we made that firm decision to completely alter the course of our lives and give them over to the Lord's service in a foreign country, a rush of concerns and questions flooded our minds.

What would be the reaction of our children?
Would our parents support us in this decision?
What would our friends say?
Where would we go?
What would we do?
How would we support ourselves?

After pausing to catch a breath from these onrushing and overwhelming questions, we realized we should bounce this decision off someone else to gauge what the reactions might be and how we might prepare to answer. That is why, I believe, God sent Dennis along with us to the retreat.

On the way home we told him our decision. Of course he was surprised. But laid-back Dennis proved to be a good trial run to test this concept out on and to help us think through some ideas and explanations during our two-hour trip back to Bloomington.

We decided to handle this just as we had done so many other things in our marriage and our lives.

Step-by-step.

One decision at a time.

One day, or maybe even one half-day, at a time.

At this time Angie had graduated from college and worked at State Farm in Bloomington. Becky lived in Champaign, Illinois, a sophomore at the University of Illinois. Sam was in sixth grade at small Towanda Elementary School, in the town closest to our rural home.

I've never experienced such an emotional time as I did in the weeks following that BSF retreat. What else could one expect after such a radical life-changing decision? By emotional, I don't mean crying or regretting our decision. Our emotions ranged from great relief for finally having made the decision to uncertainty over the reactions of others (especially close friends and relatives), fear of the unknown, and anxiety over giving up the security of a stable long-time job with great benefits.

Turmoil tore at our insides.

One of the major things we wrestled with was our finances.

After the Quest experience of 1989, Peggy and I thought someday I would take early retirement and we would be missionaries under our own agenda. We would be able to support ourselves and be somewhat independent.

But now we heard God asking us to step out in faith and simply rely on Him for our resources, including our daily bread.

CHAPTER 12

Decisions, Decisions

As we turned into our driveway that Sunday afternoon I rehearsed how I would break this news to our children.

I don't remember exactly what I said, but when the words finally tumbled out of my mouth I felt somewhat relieved. We didn't have to wait long before the barrage of questions began.

"Where are you going to go?"

"What are you going to do?"

"Which mission organization will you join?"

Angie, at one point, said, "Kids are supposed to go off to the mission field, and the parents should stay back and support them. But our parents intend to go off to the mission field and leave their kids behind!"

When we heard Angie's and Becky's questions and reservations about our decision, our thoughts raced back to 1989, at which time we had halted the process of going to the foreign mission field because of their resistance to being uprooted four or five times in the process. This time, though, Peggy and I resolved to proceed, having confidence they could make their own way in the world as independent adults.

Sam surprised all of us by saying, "If it's God's will for Mom and Dad, then we shouldn't question it." Bless his heart, because as a twelve-year-old he stood on the brink of having his life completely shaken up. Because of his age, wherever we went he would go also. He seemed comfortable with that, and we don't remember him ever arguing or balking about what lay ahead for him.

Thinking about telling our parents filled Peggy and me with anxiety. Peggy's mom, although a little hesitant, gave us her blessing and encouragement for us to proceed. My parents also hesitated but weren't completely surprised and didn't resist. With their having observed all our foreign missions trips, I'm sure they knew it was inevitable that we would someday go to the foreign field.

After informing our loved ones of our decision, the same relentless questions continued to hound us, demanding answers.

With whom?

Where?

When?

What?

And the most faith-stretching—how?

Sticking with our plan to proceed one step at a time, answering the "with whom" question topped our list of priorities.

We made a list of potential mission organizations to consider. Eventually we narrowed the list down to the following four organizations (in alphabetical order): Bible Study Fellowship (BSF), Project AmaZon (PAZ), Worldteam, and Wycliffe Bible Translators.

Our personal experiences with these organizations gave us some level of familiarity and trust as we contemplated entering into a ministry partnership with them. But, ultimately, we could join only one. We gave ourselves the immediate assignment of determining which one it should be.

We considered partnering with BSF because of our years of positive ministry experiences with them. Our understanding of the Bible and its application to our lives grew appreciably deeper through our BSF studies and leadership responsibilities. However, other than conducting BSF men's and women's studies in several foreign countries, the only mission outreach they had at the time was Rafiki. Rafiki means "friend" in Swahili. As a fledgling organization in 2000, Rafiki was setting up "self-help" villages for women and children in Tanzania and Kenya.

At that time we didn't feel called to Africa (another evidence of God's sense of humor!), and working with a small, fairly new organization sponsoring women's and children's self-help programs didn't match the desires of our hearts. So we struck BSF-Rafiki from our list.

Next to go was Worldteam. We gained much of our short-term missions experience from Worldteam through projects and mission trips in Haiti, Jamaica, St. Vincent, and Tobago. I had visited Russia with Hod Getz of Worldteam Associates. We knew many wonderful Worldteam missionaries doing a lot of good things in the Caribbean and other parts of the world. Even though we enjoyed a close relationship, something just didn't feel compatible between us and Worldteam. On our mission trips in partnership with them we never saw someone doing the exact job we wished we could be doing.

After much prayer and discussion, we were down to PAZ and Wycliffe, each with many positives. The leaders of PAZ were our close relatives, and we had followed their activities nearly all our lives. We prayed for them, we contributed financially and personally to their work, and we had been invited by them on several occasions to come and work with them. They would accommodate us well, and we would be comfortable living with them. We could even imagine just about how and where we would live.

But two things eventually turned our decision away from Santarém, Brazil. One was a result of our visit to Brazil in 1998, when we experienced a charismatic style of worship that was uncomfortable for us, given our life experiences to that point in time. And secondly and maybe more importantly, deep down I think Peggy and I were looking for something headed in a different direction, somewhere off the "beaten path," a work God had set aside special just for us.

After many days of consideration and prayer, we decided to cast our lot with Wycliffe Bible Translators, the organization that first made Peggy aware of missions, the organization we had been affiliated with in many different ways since the late 1970s.

The time period from our decision at the BSF retreat to go until our selection of Wycliffe as the organization we would go with was really quite short. God had been preparing our hearts for a long time, and I think that helped facilitate the process of making our mission organization choice without delay.

I called the headquarters of Wycliffe in Orlando, Florida, and explained our decision. They appeared to receive this news with great enthusiasm. I reminded them that we had gone through the membership application process eleven years before, and I really hoped our documents from 1989 were still in our files so we wouldn't have to redo them. We had been required to write our statements of faith and our doctrinal statements as part of our applications to join Wycliffe. Preparing these documents involved a lot of self-introspection, research, and time. My doctrinal statement had been twenty single-spaced pages and Peggy's was seventeen.

In addition to all that paperwork, we remembered as if it were yesterday all the tests, interviews, reading, and coursework from our Quest experience. The thought of redoing all our paperwork and documentation caused me a lot of anxiety as we reentered the Wycliffe application process.

The Wycliffe representative explained that they usually only keep applicants' records for ten years (for us now it had been eleven). In addition to that, they had purged a lot of records during the move of the Wycliffe headquarters from Huntington Beach, California, across the country to Orlando, Florida. He promised, though, that he would conduct a diligent search.

The very next day, much to our delight, and his, he called to say he had found our file. It was complete, and if our statements of faith, doctrinal statements, and educational achievements hadn't changed, we just needed to update our physical exams.

Our fundamental beliefs had not changed, so we simply made our doctor appointments and continued to the next step. Somewhere, somehow, God had kept our file safe and intact. We recognized this as another confirming signal from Him that we were walking the path He had prepared for us.

As we entered into discussions with Wycliffe regarding our proposed career track, I resigned myself, based on the decisions made eleven years earlier, to join them as an administrator. We did again discuss my original desire to be a translator and the denial I had received because of my age. They acknowledged the previous age restriction but in the meantime had concluded that logic was faulty, and they now had no age restrictions on translators. I had to hold my tongue as I reflected on the rigors they had put me through back in 1989.

Regardless, this time around I was prepared to be an administrator. Based on the agreement to go forward on the administration track, the Wycliffe representative informed us, "The next step for you, Gary and Peggy, is to attend MDOC [Management Development and Orientation Course] in Dallas, Texas."

"When is the next MDOC class?"

"It starts August 14th. Lasts until mid-December."

"We'll be there," we replied.

"Can you really be ready that soon?" he asked with doubt evident in his voice.

"Yep, we'll be there. When Peggy and I put our minds to something, we do everything in our power to achieve it."

We enrolled immediately.

The Wycliffe policy manual states that whichever career path the husband chooses, his wife must also receive the same training.

It seems more logical to me and a better use of resources for the husband to be chosen for his specialty and the wife for hers. This time around, though, we knew better than to question Wycliffe policy, even if we disagreed.

I chuckled at the thought of Peggy sitting with me through business administration and management courses and imagined her mind wandering to more practical homemaking tasks during our classes. But she gamely complied, sighed, and said, "Whatever it takes to be on our way!"

I believe God has a sense of humor; however, it's not always so funny at the time. As we were undergoing the difficult processes of determining which organization to cast our lot with, quitting a comfortable job, leaving two of our children behind, anticipating being overseas for extended periods of time and all the other upcoming disruptions to our lives, the director of another division at State Farm Insurance called me into his office one day.

After closing his office door he said, "I'm planning to propose to upper management for you to join my department. I like your style, and I think this could really be a good advancement opportunity for you. I have discussed this with your director, but no one else knows. So please keep this under your hat for the time being. What do you think?"

Honestly, I felt as if someone had just knocked the wind out of me. I couldn't breathe.

I had not yet told State Farm of our intention to go into full-time mission work. I am sure this man anticipated that I would jump at the opportunity and immediately say "yes." With my mind racing over all the upcoming tough decisions and major life changes I was facing, I couldn't bring myself to say either "no" or "yes."

I said, "Let me think it over and get back to you in the next couple of days."

"Okay."

I agonized over this decision. There was no way I could go back on my commitment to become a missionary. After all we had been through, it was clear that leaving my job and pursuing full-time missions was God's will. But if it was His will, why was He testing me like this?

To accept the transfer was extremely tempting. The new job would likely come with a better salary and other benefits. Remaining at State Farm in a new job would be so much easier than facing a huge upheaval in my life.

"Why? Why? Why at this time, Lord?"

Telling Peggy of the attractive offer brought no sympathy from her. She reminded me, "God has clearly showed us His will. We've made the decision. We've told our kids and both sides of our family, as well as our friends. I thought we were agreed that this is what we wanted to do. So why even spend even one minute considering this offer? It's just a distraction."

I returned to the director's office the next day. "Can I ask you to also keep something confidential? I really appreciate your confidence in me and your generous offer. However, my wife and I are going to become full-time missionaries. We will be working with an organization involved in Bible translation for those people who don't yet have the Word of God in their language. I will soon be announcing my resignation from State Farm. Please don't tell anyone yet."

He responded, "Wow, I never expected an answer like that! I understand. Good luck."

It wasn't easy, but after it was over, it felt so good to have made the right decision. Overcoming that difficult temptation bolstered my faith, and I felt ready for any test of my commitment. But I had no idea what challenges still lay ahead.

CHAPTER 13

Preparations

I'm amazed how my attitude toward my house, my castle, changed over time. In 1986 we built our dream home in a rural subdivision two miles from the little town of Towanda, Illinois, a bedroom community of Bloomington-Normal.

Stately elm and walnut trees graced the front part of the corner lot we had purchased two years prior to the start of construction. A steep hill in the wooded back half led down to a creek running through the rear of the lot.

As the general contractors, Peggy and I designed the floor plan and selected all the fixtures, cabinets, windows, and all the hundreds of other items required. We hired the subcontractors, but we also did a huge amount of the work ourselves.

I clearly remember thinking, after we had moved into that beautiful house, "This really is our dream home. Everything is just perfect for our family."

But, alas, the very next year God blessed us with another child, our son, Sam. (Not alas that he was born, but alas, my dream house was no longer perfect!) Each of our daughters had her own bedroom, but now baby brother needed a place to sleep. Having no extra bedrooms, we built a bedroom in the basement for Angie.

We had a three-car garage designed for our car, pickup truck, and riding mower. Then Angie got a car. So we built a storage shed to accommodate the riding mower. Three years later Becky turned sixteen and got a car. Now what?

Thus, our "perfect home" of 1986 only accommodated our dreams for a short time. As humans, we don't foresee the changes that come and upset our "best-laid" plans. We don't like to admit it, but it invariably happens. Even though our dream home changed dramatically over the years, our family enjoyed a lot of wonderful memories there and became quite attached to it. But we could not possibly keep that house while living full-time overseas, perhaps halfway around the world. We had to sell our beloved home!

Deciding to sell that home was a hard decision, but it needed to be done. I painted a For Sale sign, but I needed several days to get up the courage to stake it out in the yard. When I finally mustered the courage, I drove the stakes of the sign into the ground late in the evening, thinking no one would see me. In spite of my caution, a couple did walk by as I hammered. They asked me what I was doing, and for the first time I publicly uttered the words "We're selling our home."

Those words got caught somewhere in my throat.

Contrary to many neighborhoods today, we knew all our neighbors, and we knew them well. As one of the first families to build a house in that subdivision, we watched with anticipation as each subsequent house was built. We met nearly every family as they moved into their new houses. Reminiscent of the times our parents grew up in, we helped each other out in time of need, coached each other's kids in soccer and baseball, loaned tools back and forth, and talked over the proverbial "back fence," although no one had fences. We anguished over the thought of leaving that comfortable neighborhood and our good friends.

In addition to the angst of leaving our neighborhood, I also wrestled with leaving my job. I was halfway through my 26th year of employment at State Farm when we decided to become full-time missionaries. After that long period of employment, I had acquired a lot of benefits, including a good salary, medical and dental insurance, a 401(k) plan, a retirement plan fully funded by the company, credit union benefits, free employee physical exams, educational incentives, regular raises, paid vacation, and personal time off.

Resigning from State Farm at age fifty-one meant all of those benefits flew out the window except the 401(k) account and someday in the future a reduced retirement benefit. Everything else would disappear—vaporize into thin air.

Those kinds of perks are known as "golden handcuffs" for a good reason. I struggled with removing them from my own wrists. When I asked myself how in the world I could replace those benefits from my own pocket on a missionary's income, I realized I couldn't, even though I spent a few sleepless nights trying to figure out how to do it.

In the years following our attempt to join Wycliffe in 1989, I began to imagine that someday after I was eligible to take early retirement I would retire and go into full-time mission work according to my own agenda. That thought seemed comfortable and reassuring, and it dangled safely off somewhere in the future.

Now that I faced the possibility of resignation before eligibility for retirement, doubts and second-guessing wormed their way into my mind. I started asking myself, "I'm just a central Illinois farm boy; what difference can I really make in the big world?"

"Is this God's will?"

"Did I really hear Him call?"

Understanding that these thoughts undoubtedly reeked of Satan trying to discourage me, I determined through prayer, time in God's Word, and sheer resolve to stay the course I felt God had called Peggy and me to travel.

As we continued our preparations, we received some very wise advice to keep a house that we could come home to when we returned from overseas on furlough or vacation. Many missionaries sell off everything, including their homes, planning to stay with parents or friends during furlough time. In most cases that works for a while. But for a longer stay, the true words of an old saying manifest themselves: "After three days, both fish and guests start to smell."

Peggy and I, fortunately, followed the advice to maintain a home in the U.S. Peggy took on the task of finding a condominium or similar type of house to downsize to. Having such a place would give us not only somewhere to stay when we came back to Illinois (although that seemed at the time to be way off in the future) but also a place to keep things we wanted to save. We reasoned that unless we died on the mission field, eventually circumstances would bring us back to the United States. By maintaining a home stateside we would also be prepared with furniture and appliances when God led us to return.

Another reason this is a good idea is that housing costs continue to escalate over time. If one sells a house and puts the proceeds in the bank, it is highly unlikely that the amount of money in the bank will buy anything substantial many years later when the missionary is again ready to take up residence in his home country. Keeping a stateside home while overseas is a hedge against housing price inflation.

Peggy spent countless hours driving all over Bloomington-Normal with a realtor looking at townhouses, condos, apartments, duplexes, you-name-it. When she found one with potential, we went to look at it together and discussed whether it was a good fit or not. After a lot of time and effort on her part, she finally found the house we decided to buy.

While not exactly the dream home we had built fourteen years before, it met our needs. Located back in the city of Bloomington, the duplex shares a common lot line with its identical, but mirror-image, twin next door. It requires some outside landscaping and yard maintenance throughout the year, but there are no maintenance fees or homeowners' association charges.

As we searched for a home to downsize to, we weren't having any luck selling our other house on our own. Since we didn't want an empty house-for-sale hanging over our heads as we went off to be missionaries, we eventually listed our home with a realtor.

Only a small fraction of our possessions would fit into our new home. We accepted that fact and sold many of our things by word of mouth and advertisements in the newspaper. In addition, we watched strangers carry our earthly treasures away from a giant garage sale.

Eventually we realized we needed outside help to sell off the large amount of household goods that were still left over. We con-tracted with an auction house in my hometown of Fairbury to take everything left from the garage sale to sell on auction.

Another necessary preparation for leaving for the mission field was raising financial support. Raising support is probably the most feared and disliked thing about becoming a faith-based missionary. Peggy and I always prided ourselves on our independence. In 1999 leading up to the Y2K (Year 2000) potential meltdown of our society, we had drilled a well for water on our lot, put away extra food, bought a generator, stored up gasoline, and thought through all the things we needed to do to survive the upcoming "disaster."

Asking our friends and relatives for financial support not only caused us a lot of anxiety but also greatly humbled us. We prepared a letter explaining our intentions in conjunction with God's leading as well as envelopes for nearly 400 friends and relatives. God's ironical sense of humor manifested itself again, as He watched us humbly admit we couldn't do this alone.

Peggy's sister and brother-in-law generously allowed us to use their house in Breckenridge, Colorado, for a week of vacation in June. While our kids had a good time in and around Breckenridge, Peggy and I prepared all those letters, writing personal notes on each one.

Following a prayer over the huge stack of envelopes, we sent them off in the mail. After several weeks of holding our breath and pleading with God to touch the hearts of those we had written to, we received an e-mail from Wycliffe in July that gave us the initial results. We felt there must have been a mistake; we couldn't believe our eyes. From our supporters we had received $11,185. This huge amount of money significantly exceeded our expectations. We felt so blessed, humbled, and encouraged to continue our journey.

The next month, as expected, our support funds fell off to about half that, and beyond that it settled down into the $2,000 to $3,000 per month range. God had provided for an amazing start to the frightening process of raising funds.

Even though raising support was a tremendously humbling exercise, it has turned out to be great blessing. Not only financially, but in so many other gracious and generous ways, people have come alongside us to help. God truly uses a team to support missionaries who place their trust in Him.

When we received that e-mail from Wycliffe, we no longer had to pinch ourselves to be reminded that we were on the road to overseas missions. But we had not yet reached the point of no return. We could still call the whole thing off. But after so many clear signs and confirmations from God, could we possibly dare to do so?

CHAPTER 14

Final Days Before Departure

As August 8, 2000 (our scheduled departure date for Dallas), approached, our house still hadn't sold. Our anxiety level was escalating. That house and yard required a lot of attention and work. We knew it could not sit empty and still be maintained properly after we moved out. Failure to find a buyer really discouraged us. The God who had shown His awesome presence in so many other aspects of our lives seemed to have forgotten our concern over the upkeep of the house and the urgent need for the money from it to buy our condo and pay off our other debts as well.

When our little condo in Bloomington was nearly finished, we moved everything we planned to keep into that house. As with any new house, decisions about final touches nagged at us. The list of "things-to-do" rose in urgency because of our intention to be gone for so long. We offered Angie the opportunity to live in the condo during our absence. Because our downsized condo meant an upsize from her tiny apartment, and because we offered it rent-free, she seized the opportunity to move in and be the caretaker. The benefits of that deal went both ways. Our minds were at ease knowing she would give our new home a lived-in appearance and tender loving care.

In addition to the outstanding issue of needing to sell our previous home, we also had to deal with the question of what to do with our beloved dog. When we first moved into our rural home fourteen years before, the kids begged for a dog. They also wanted cats. And cats, being so independent, are easy. However, a dog requires much more care and attention. Peggy and I both grew up on farms where it was a given that people live inside the house and animals live outside the house. We solidly agreed on that but needed to make sure our daughters also understood.

Once we had their agreement that a dog would live outside, Peggy and the girls went dog-shopping. They ended up at an animal shelter in Chenoa, Illinois, about twenty miles away. Their little hearts couldn't bear the thought that an adorable cocker spaniel doggie was going to be put to sleep the next day. They brought her home, exuding love for our new family member, who they had rescued from the Grim Reaper. Because of her close brush with death, we named her Lucky.

We didn't know Lucky's age when she joined us, but now, fourteen years later, she was still plodding along as an integral family member. We couldn't imagine how she survived so long. She did not get to come into the house, but on bitter cold nights I had sympathy for her and allowed her to sleep in the garage under a heat lamp.

Part of the family, always there, always wagging her little cocker spaniel tail, she greeted us every morning as we emerged from the house. But signs of her advanced age were showing. She couldn't hear very well any more and had several cysts that needed to be surgically removed. For the previous three years I had told the kids she would never make it through another winter, but every spring she was still wagging that tail to greet me in the mornings.

During that spring and summer, as we prepared to move, we prayed we would wake up some morning and find that Lucky had peacefully gone off to "doggie heaven" during the night. But it didn't happen. She couldn't live inside our new condo, and the tiny yard there was way too restrictive for her after fourteen years of roaming her large domain.

So, at the last possible moment, with Lucky still not having gone off to her eternal home, Peggy and I tried to convince each other to take her to the veterinarian to "put her to sleep."

Oh my, that was tough!

Eventually the task fell upon my shoulders. I lifted Lucky up into the back of my pickup truck, and off we went. When I got to the veterinarian's office, a young lady came out to get her. I told her I didn't even want Lucky's leash back, as I didn't want any memento of that terrible day.

Time marched resolutely on, and soon it was time for the auction house to come and get our unsold household goods. Our hearts broke to see all our possessions being carted away in the auctioneer's trailer like so much junk. In reality, though, that's what our earthly treasures are. The gospel of Matthew is one of several places in the Bible where Jesus instructs His followers not to love the things of this world and not to crave the accumulation of those things "where moth and rust destroy, and where thieves break in and steal" (Matthew 6:19 NIV). In spite of that, we will be the first to say that it's not easy to let go of material things. They are nothing compared to what our mansions in heaven will be furnished with. In spite of understanding that principle, it still was really hard to see those things go.

Peggy and I went to Fairbury to watch our things sell on auction. That turned out to be a terrible idea. Our "precious treasures" sold for only pennies on the dollar. A chair in perfect condition that we paid $400 for sold for $25. Other things we had used or treasured for years were practically being given away. At that point Peggy wanted to start buying things back. With really heavy hearts we left that awful place in our rearview mirrors long before the auction was over.

Our house still sat on the market unsold.

We had just put our dear doggie to sleep.

Our earthly possessions had been treated like discarded rubbish.

We still had a lot of work to do to prepare our condo for us being gone for nearly two years.

We were leaving our loved ones.

We had no idea which country we would end up in.

We were sad and depressed.

On the way to our condo from the auction, we stopped at our rural home to pick up the last few things remaining there. After loading them onto our pickup we said another sad "good-bye" to that house and headed out of the subdivision. As we passed the rear of our lot we saw a car parked in a lane at the back of our property. Thinking it a little strange, I stopped to investigate.

Two people, Bobby and Elaine Mueller, emerged from the woods. Bobby is a first cousin to my dad.

We exchanged greetings, and I asked, "What in the world are you guys doing here?"

"We're waiting on a realtor—we came to look at your house."

"Well, it's still our house, so we can show you around. Come on in," we replied, with eagerness probably too evident in our voices.

We showed them our house, and they asked a lot of questions. They looked in detail at everything. Many potential buyers had been turned off at Peggy's choice of carpet colors, wallpaper, and wood stains. They wanted everything to be neutral colors. But Bobby and Elaine said they liked our decorating. At the end of the house tour, Bobby said he would call on Monday to let us know what they decided. That meant we would wait in suspense for two days.

Monday came, and Bobby did call. "Hey, Gary, we really like your house, but I need to talk to my lawyer. Hopefully I can give you a call tomorrow."

On Tuesday he called back and said, "Everything's okay; we want to buy your home. The offer will be coming through the realtors."

I asked, "If we accept your offer, can your lawyer make the closing happen within a week? We have to leave for Dallas a week from today." I also called our attorney and asked if a closing could happen within one week because of our time crunch.

Fortunately, the lawyers were friends and agreed to cooperate to have the closing the following Wednesday. This meant postponing our departure one day. Even though we settled for a few thousand dollars less than we had asked, we were elated. Truly, God answered our prayers in an amazing way, but once again according to His timetable. We are not privy to His timing, probably because if we were, faith would not be required. At that juncture, Peggy and I felt our faith was being tested to the max.

Things were definitely starting to look up. We were ascending out of the pit of despair. I could readily relate to David's psalms. One day, like him, I could write laments from the pit; the next, I wanted to find a harp and join him in his psalms of rejoicing on the mountaintop. Peggy and I were not the only humans to spend time doing both; the greatest king of Israel did so likewise.

I left my office at State Farm for the last time on August 1, the day Bobby called, offering to buy our house. That gave us exactly one week to work on our new house until we left. We worked hard on our condo that week—landscaping, organizing, and preparing our possessions for our absence. We closed on our Towanda home, as agreed, on Wednesday, August 9, in the morning. Our realtor, knowing our plans to drive both our car and pickup truck to Dallas, blessed us with three walkie-talkies with a range of two miles to keep us connected in those days before everyone had a cell phone. This proved extremely valuable for Peggy, Sam, and me to keep track of each other on the way to Texas.

After the closing we met our kids at Hardee's fast food restaurant for a quick lunch together. With a lot of sad good-byes—the first of many more to come—we headed south. Peggy drove the car, and I drove the truck, and Sam alternated between the two.

When we arrived in Texas it was 104 degrees F (40 degrees C).

CHAPTER 15

Dallas, Texas

It was so hot. The Dallas area was in the midst of record-breaking drought and heat. Those suffering souls had gone eighty-some days without rain, and every day the temperature exceeded 100 degrees Fahrenheit (38 C). Without any exaggeration, by the time we finished hanging a load of laundry on the clothesline, the first items we hung up were already dry.

For the first time in my life I experienced 112 degree F (44 C) temperatures, and I wondered how people in even hotter locales could survive. Hot hardly described the weather; blistering comes closer.

Due to the house closing back in Illinois, we arrived in Dallas (actually a suburb of Dallas named Duncanville) a day later than we had planned, leaving us with less than four days until Sam started school. Moving the few things we brought with us into our small apartment didn't take long. Fortunately our apartment had a struggling air conditioner.

On our first day in Duncanville we met another couple in our apartment complex, Bill and Glenna Brewington (and their son, Martin), who were enrolled in our same MDOC class. Martin was also in seventh grade, so he and Sam were going to be classmates as well as neighbors. Right away we learned two things from the Brewingtons—first, they were planning to go to Kenya after

MDOC (this will be significant later), and second, there was a dress code for Duncanville Junior High School (this was significant immediately).

The mandatory dress code allowed the boys to wear only red, white, and blue shirts with collars. It also limited the colors of long slacks to navy, khaki, and black. Absolutely no T-shirts, shorts, or blue jeans were permitted. The clothes could have no logos or writing on them.

Desperately we sorted through all of Sam's clothes that we had brought with us. Not one piece of his clothing met the dress code—not one! With two days to go until school started, and being in entirely unfamiliar surroundings, Peggy raced out to shop for Sam's clothes. She looked in every store in our neighborhood and found nothing. Then we realized all the local families had already bought up all the clothes meeting the dress code, leaving nothing for us.

With only one day left to find appropriate clothes for Sam, Peggy drove to other Dallas suburbs and finally found some clothes that worked. Over time we were able to add to Sam's wardrobe, but what an introduction to our new community!

Back at Towanda Elementary School Sam had had twenty classmates. In Duncanville he had hundreds. Many big adjustments challenged our son, but he successfully met all of them head-on and adapted well. We were proud to watch him head off to school each day with a positive attitude, knowing he was undergoing a big cultural shock for a young kid.

In our new neighborhood we found several mega-churches. On several occasions we visited Tony Evans' church—Oak Cliff Bible Church—which was located right down the road from our apartment. Having been raised in the Apostolic Christian Church meant we wore suits, white shirts, and ties to church on Sunday. Now, far from home and in the scorching Dallas heat, I figured the dress code would lighten up a little. Again, God's sense of humor kicked in. As we walked into that nearly 100 percent black church, we felt underdressed in comparison to everyone else. Men wore suits and ties, and the ladies accented their beautiful dresses with hats and gloves.

Peggy and I started MDOC, meeting our new classmates and instructors. We soaked up the goals and objectives of the course. But, most of all, we eagerly anticipated that time in November when we would learn our assignments and where in the world we would serve. That added a thrill, some jitters, and anticipation to our syllabus.

The semester brought lots of course work on all kinds of management issues—personnel, government relations, budgets, organizational structure, intercultural communications, security, and on and on. It reminded me of my MBA graduate work, only in a completely different context. In addition to the regular classroom studies and homework, we each had two large additional responsibilities, which included a semester-long major project and an assignment working in an actual office situation.

Together my advisor and I developed a semester-long project for me to write a paper entitled "Developing and Maintaining Financial Well-Being within Wycliffe Bible Translators." The paper documented six major areas of a Wycliffe member's financial health, which I identified as active duty income, income tax planning, investment planning, insurance, retirement planning, and estate planning. My concern over how to replace these financial benefits from my State Farm days triggered my interest in a missionary's financial health—especially my own.

The project Peggy selected fit her to a tee—she elected to write a recipe book. She realized that it would not be possible to take her large collection of recipe books to our foreign assignment, so she wanted to assemble a collection of all of the best recipes she could find. She wrote to her friends and relatives, asking for their favorite recipes. If she remembered something really good from somewhere or someone, she wrote and asked for the recipe. Of course, she added her own favorites. She entitled the book Simply Delicious.

Setting it up in book format on the computer, she tediously laid out each page. Following that she took it to the SIL print shop and had it published. She still uses that recipe book to this day and gave away many copies as gifts. Given its popularity, she should have printed many more copies.

For my office assignment I was asked to work each afternoon in the office of the SIL finance vice-president. The VP gave me a really nice office with a computer, secretary, and the whole works. I met with the vice-president on a few occasions initially, but shortly after I started he took off for an extended stretch at Wycliffe headquarters in Orlando, Florida, leaving me in charge of the SIL finance office in Dallas. He called every day with instructions, requests, and updates. Impressed with the responsibility he had given to such an unproven staff member, I felt a little awkward and intimidated dealing with the full-time employees who couldn't understand who I was to come in and take over. I honestly didn't understand it either, but I appreciated the opportunity and learned a lot through practical experience.

Peggy assisted the personnel director, a former missionary to South America, with data entry on the computer.

As promised, in November we MDOC students received permission to start the process of determining the country of our eventual overseas assignment. We were given the guidelines and received the go-ahead to immediately start contacting SIL branch offices around the world. Although our instructors gave us a list of known job openings, we learned that the list might be either incomplete or out-of-date. Therefore, if we desired to serve in any particular country without a position available on the list or if we wanted a certain type of position, we could contact the branches and inquire whether such an opportunity had presented itself in the interim.

Before we started the process, Peggy and I made a short list of our requirements and constraints. Peggy said she was willing to go anywhere except India or Africa. (God smiled about that one.) We also wanted to go to a country where Sam could live with us while he attended school, rather than having to attend boarding school in another country. (God also smiled about that one.) And we wanted to go where there was the greatest need.

Down deep, Peggy just knew we would go to Papua New Guinea (PNG). She had always been attracted to PNG, especially after hearing missionaries from there speak at Wycliffe Associates banquets. And I felt that if we didn't go to one of the former Soviet satellite countries, we would end up nearby at one of the "-stan" countries, like Pakistan or Kazakhstan. That probably originated from my interest in the former Soviet republics and was strengthened by our trip to Eastern Europe in 1985 and my subsequent trip to Russia in 1996. My interest in the "-stan" countries was further motivated by the push by mission organizations for missionaries to serve in Muslim countries. Some missionaries I talked to had made it sound very adventuresome and fulfilling.

With those few constraints we set out on the quest to determine our destiny. We read everything we could find on various countries and people groups, asked a lot of questions of SIL missionaries, researched online, and sent lots of e-mails to various SIL branch offices around the world.

In addition, various entities within SIL and Wycliffe recruited us to come to their offices. I received a strong pitch to join the government relations branches in New York and Washington, D.C. Although tempted, we were determined to go overseas.

We found little opportunity in South America, as most of the necessary translations were being wrapped up and SIL was withdrawing from many of those countries. Our search eventually narrowed down to some Pacific islands (including PNG, along with Vanuatu and the Solomon Islands), Asia, and several of the Eastern

European "-stan" countries. Africa technically remained off-limits, as Peggy was adamant about not going there, in spite of the urging of some newfound missionary friends.

At Dallas we met a young lady from our Apostolic Christian Church in Bluffton, Indiana, by the name of Kami Isch. Kami had taught in Cameroon for two years at the Wycliffe school and tried diligently to convince us to consider selecting Cameroon as our foreign assignment. Another couple, our MDOC classmates, were missionaries in Cameroon and also tried to persuade us to go to that West African country. Peggy told all of them that Africa was off the board.

Our counselor, Esther Steen, a veteran of many, many years of being an overseas missionary, oversaw our search and helped us a great deal. We enjoyed working with her, as she had a very empathetic spirit.

After several weeks of phone calls, prayer, and e-mailing, we took her our list. She looked it over and commented, "I don't see Kenya on your list."

We responded, "Well, you know, we have that thing about not wanting to go to India or Africa."

With tears glistening in her eyes, she explained, "You know, my husband and I served many years in Kenya. He was gored and killed by a buffalo and is buried over there. I have real attachment to that country."

(By the way, the African buffalo is one of the nastiest creatures God ever put on earth. It looks like an overgrown cow, but that is where the similarity ends.)

We relented, "Okay, we will add Kenya to our list."

And later to each other we said, "If we're going to allow Kenya on our list, we have no excuse for not adding Cameroon for Kami."

We wrote to the Cameroon and Kenya offices, telling of our availability and inquiring about open branch administration positions. Kenya answered right away with an e-mail saying they would welcome us; however, they wondered if we would consider going to Ethiopia, where they needed the greatest amount of administrative help.

This Africa thing was getting out of control!

I wrote to the Ethiopia branch and immediately received two of the warmest invitation letters of our entire search process. Mary Breeze, the branch director, answered all our questions in detail and explained even more than we asked about the branch. Hilleen Middleton, the personnel director, also wrote a very encouraging and helpful e-mail response to us. Those two ladies seemed to be genuinely interested in our going to Ethiopia.

Shortly thereafter we again approached Esther, this time with our new and shorter list. It now read:

Papua New Guinea
Cameroon
Kenya
Ethiopia

In all of those countries Sam could live with us at home while attending school. Only our first constraint, about not going to India or Africa, had been violated (to this point).

A day or two later, Bill and Glenna Brewington (the first classmates we met when we arrived in Duncanville and the ones who told us they were going to Kenya) came into the classroom excited about the fact that God had revealed to them where they should go. They looked relieved, remarking, "God has shown us without a doubt our foreign assignment."

"Well, duh, you've always said you're going to Kenya! So it's Kenya, right?"

"That's changed; we're going to Papua New Guinea," Glenna enthusiastically replied.

I nearly fell out of my chair, and Peggy's heart sank. The leaders of MDOC had informed us at the beginning of the term that, unless God had without a doubt called us to a certain country, two families from our class would not go to the same place. This guideline was put into place because of the scarcity of trained administration personnel around the world.

And so, haltingly, we struck our number-one choice, Papua New Guinea, from our list. God, chuckling on His throne, watched us gaze at our short list of three African countries. Nothing promising had come from my research on former Soviet countries or the "-stans."

We then faced the difficult task of deciding among Kenya, Ethiopia, or Cameroon. Our advisers told us the Africa area director, the person in charge of all SIL activities in Africa (based in Nairobi, Kenya), Dan Butler, was coming to Dallas in the next week. I quickly e-mailed him, asking if we could meet with him during his stay in Dallas. He agreed, and we scheduled lunch together.

During lunch we quickly reviewed our situation with him and asked, "Since we are trying to decide among these three African countries—Kenya, Ethiopia, and Cameroon—can you tell us which has the greatest need for administrative help?"

He answered, "I am the director of all SIL activities in Africa. I cannot be partial to any one branch."

We continued eating. Again we brought the subject around to where the greatest need was. And again he responded as he did previously.

After about two hours, he looked at his watch and said, "Boy, I really need to get back to my meeting. It's getting late."

"Okay, Dan, just one more question."

"And what is that?"

"Which of those branches has the greatest need for our help?"

He smiled and answered, "Well, the greatest need is in Ethiopia. They really need your help."

And we replied, "Okay, then, we'll go to Ethiopia."

For Peggy and me that moment's significance ranks right up there with our wedding and the decision to become full-time overseas missionaries. The magnitude of what we had just said didn't really sink in until much later. But the die was cast!

As we left our training building that day, we met the man in charge of security of SIL personnel around the world. He worries about wars, hurricanes, riots, earthquakes, coups, and any other thing that could place a missionary in harm's way.

We asked, "Sir, what do you know about Ethiopia? We seem to have just made the decision to work at the Ethiopia branch office."

"Well, they are just concluding a nasty two-year war with Eritrea. And, of course, you understand that Ethiopia is known for famine, HIV-AIDS, extreme poverty, and all that. But I was just in Ethiopia, and it is a beautiful country with warm people. Addis Ababa is probably the safest capital city in all of Africa."

Then he pulled out some pictures of his trip to Ethiopia from his briefcase and showed them to us. This apparently was to substantiate his encouragement for us to strongly consider Ethiopia. He enthusiastically pointed out every detail of the photographs.

After leaving him, we rushed home to tell Sam he was going to Ethiopia. We also couldn't wait to let our daughters and parents know we had made our huge decision.

We felt relieved and excited but now very curious and apprehensive about what was in store for us. It is nearly impossible to describe all the emotions that welled up within Peggy and me. Prior to that day, going off to some faraway foreign field was merely a concept, a romantic tale to relate to others. We could imagine the steaming jungles of Papua New Guinea, the steppes of Ukraine, or the Vietnamese culture I had heard so much about during my army service, but now my thoughts turned to acacia trees, big animals, and a country of black people. As a man not accustomed to showing a lot of emotion, I almost couldn't handle the excitement, anticipation, and sheer terror looming ahead of us.

On that day our dream became reality, revolving around a place I could actually pinpoint on a map. All our preparation and prayers and the year-long roller coaster ride we had been on now focused on one location.

Ethiopia.

It was in Africa, right?

Wars, the famine of 1984-85, HIV and AIDS, grinding poverty. Had we made the correct decision? What would our friends, relatives, parents, and others say?

Could we survive Ethiopia?

CHAPTER 16

Preparations for Ethiopia

We woke up the next morning wondering what we had done to ourselves.

Were we still dreaming?

Or was it a nightmare?

Or was it for real?

As we swept the remaining cobwebs of sleep from our brains we could hardly believe we had decided to commit our lives to Ethiopia. Would our family and friends support us in this decision, or would they think we had completely lost our sanity?

When we told my parents of God's leading us to Ethiopia, my Dad surprised us by saying something like, "Well, Ethiopia, that's not so bad—after all, it's mentioned in the Bible."

In fact it is mentioned many times. In the King James Version, the name Ethiopia is almost always used when referring to the upper Nile River region where Ethiopia is located today. In other versions the translators often refer to the area as Cush. Among Christians, perhaps the best known story regarding Ethiopia is the story of Philip and the eunuch in Acts 8. As a matter of fact, practically every Ethiopian Christian is convinced that is how Christianity was introduced to their country in the first century A.D.

Ethiopia is referred to from the very creation of the earth up until the time of the disciples after Jesus ascended to heaven. Here are just a few of the references:

> Ethiopia was part of the Garden of Eden: "And the name of the second river is Gihon: the same is it that compasseth the whole land of Ethiopia" (Genesis 2:13 KJV). (The name Gihon, now usually transliterated as "Ghion," is still a common place name in Ethiopia today.)
>
> Moses' wife, Zipporah, was an Ethiopian: "And Miriam and Aaron spake against Moses because of the Ethiopian woman whom he had married: for he had married an Ethiopian woman" (Numbers 12:1 KJV).
>
> The Persian Empire was so great that it even included Ethiopia in Africa: "Now it came to pass in the days of Ahasuerus, (this is Ahasuerus which reigned, from India even unto Ethiopia, over an hundred and seven and twenty provinces:)" (Esther 1:1 KJV).
>
> The book of Job says this about "wisdom" and "understanding": "The topaz of Ethiopia shall not equal it, neither shall it be valued with pure gold" (Job 28:19).
>
> "Ethiopia shall soon stretch out her hands unto God" (Psalm 68:31 KJV).
>
> The likelihood of an evildoer doing good deeds is likened to this possibility: "Can the Ethiopian change his skin, or the leopard his spots?" (Jeremiah 13:23).
>
> And of course, as mentioned above, the well-known story of Philip's encounter with the Ethiopian eunuch: "And he arose and went: and, behold, a man of Ethiopia, an eunuch of great authority under Candace queen of the Ethiopians, who had the charge of all her treasure, and had come to Jerusalem for to worship" (Acts 8:27 KJV).

Add to these the the story that every Ethiopian child learns early-on about the Queen of Sheba being from Ethiopia (modern day Axum in the far north of the country). The familiar story relates that the Queen of Sheba went to Jerusalem to see King Solomon (we know this part to be true, because it's in the Bible). While there, she became pregnant by Solomon and gave birth to a son, Menelik, after returning to Ethiopia. As a child Menelik went back to Jerusalem for training in the courts of his father. At around age twenty he returned to Ethiopia and became king, beginning an unbroken lineage from the tribe of Judah until communist rebels deposed Emperor Haile Selassie from the throne in 1974.

Knowing we would be moving to Ethiopia, Peggy and I wanted to learn everything we could about the country and its people. I looked in the Dallas phone book and found a phone number and address for the Ethiopian Evangelical Church. Taking a bold step we called the church to find the time for the Sunday service. We visited the following Sunday morning.

Some surprises awaited us. First, we were the only white people there. Second, the people were all speaking another language, which we now know to be Amharic. Fortunately for us, most of the people also spoke English. All were friendly and made us feel very welcome. They ushered us into the sanctuary and provided us with headphones, through which we heard an English translation of the service.

After the service, our new friends directed us to the church bookstore, where we bought a New Testament with English and Amharic side by side. One man even gave us our first quick lesson in Amharic, teaching us about the seven different types of the "B" sound. The church members were excited to hear we were going to Ethiopia as missionaries. They competed with each other to tell us everything about their country.

One lady from the congregation invited us to lunch with her at an Ethiopian restaurant. As we neared the restaurant, we noticed that the store signs and even the street signs were in Amharic.

The lady ordered lunch for us—a collection of different kinds of meat, vegetables, and lentil sauces on a flat, spongy sourdough-tasting bread. Today we know these sauces as different kinds of wats (whut), and the bread is called injera (en jae ruh). When the collection of wats is served on the injera it is known as beyeaenetu (beh yeh eye neh too). Our new friend instructed us to wash our hands, because within minutes we would be eating with our fingers. All the taste sensations were very new to us, and the idea of eating with our fingers was quite strange, indeed.

A few days later two other members of that Ethiopian church came to our little apartment dressed in traditional Ethiopian clothes and explained a lot about Ethiopia and its culture. We received many impromptu lessons on our new country, and we eagerly soaked up everything we could.

Soon it was the middle of December; Sam finished his semester of school, and we graduated from MDOC. We packed our vehicles and said our good-byes. We had gone to Dallas with great expectations of being foreign missionaries but with no idea of our overseas destination. Now we were leaving Dallas knowing our destination but with lots of anxiety about going back to Illinois and on to Africa.

The day we left it sleeted! We had arrived in Dallas four months before in 104 degree heat in the midst of a searing drought. When we left it was bitterly cold with freezing rain, which accompanied us all the way back to Illinois. I wore out the windshield wiper blades on my pickup and had to stop to buy new ones and change them along the way. The poor visibility caused us to drive extremely slowly, and we returned to Bloomington exhausted.

The immediacy of our leaving Illinois to go far away for a long time now stared us and our family squarely in the face. Christmas in Ohio with Peggy's family was a time of difficult farewells. After the Christmas meal was devoured and the gifts unwrapped, Peggy's family had a very special commissioning service for us. All of

Peggy's brothers and sisters and in-laws laid hands on us and prayed. Their special display of love demonstrated genuine support and concern for us, and we reflected on that occasion many times over the ensuing months and years.

We booked our airline tickets, confirmed logistics (guest house, meals, transportation) over in Ethiopia, packed and repacked, reviewed our lists, checking them twice, and the short time remaining in the U.S. flew by.

CHAPTER 17

Ethiopia and East Africa

January 20, 2001, was the day of President George W. Bush's first inauguration. For Peggy and me the day also marked the beginning of a new era. The next day, brimming with anxiety and anticipation, we left for Ethiopia and started our African missionary journey.

We drove to Chicago's O'Hare Airport, accompanied by Peggy's sister and brother-in-law, Cindy and Darl Schieler, and our daughters. Also accompanying us were the essentials we needed for Wycliffe's field training course and for setting up our new home. We said sad farewells and boarded the Lufthansa jet.

Upon arrival in Frankfurt, Germany, we were at first surprised to see so many black people at our departure gate. Then it dawned on us that they were Ethiopians flying to the same place we were going. After engaging several Ethiopians in conversation, we found them to be as warm and accommodating as the Ethiopians we had met at the church in Dallas.

As we continued our journey from Germany, flying over Sudan and Ethiopia at night, the ground was completely dark. We saw no bright city lights along the way. This, without a doubt, was Africa, the "Dark Continent."

When the pilot announced our approach to Addis Ababa, I had one of the sickest feelings in my gut that I had ever had in my life. Satan was making an all-out attempt to attack me both physically and emotionally.

I sensed him challenging me, He asked, "Why in the world are you taking your wife and son to this place? What do you think you're going to do? Why, you've never even visited this country, nor even this continent, before!"

In my heart I replied, "But my uncle Melvin Huber went to Brazil with little preparation, and look how successful he has been. I've been through a lot of training, and God clearly showed us this is what we should do."

"Do you actually think you are on the same level as your Uncle Melvin? What about your girls back in the U.S.? Do you really think they can fend for themselves? Are you sure you heard God correctly, or did you just dream this up yourself? Didn't wiser and older people like your parents and your church leaders advise against this outrageous idea?"

Back and forth I wrestled with these thoughts and with the devil. Beyond the point of no return, there really was nothing I could do but continue the journey we had embarked on.

That heavy feeling sat in my stomach, pressing me down, until we landed and had to be about the business of clearing immigration and customs. The three of us gathered our luggage and traversed the customs bureaucracy with only few questions about the contents of our luggage. Much to our relief, across the street (the public could not enter the airport terminal) George Ellison and Jaap Haasnoot, Wycliffe members from the U.S. and the Netherlands respectively, waited for us in George's van.

We finally were in Africa. It was the middle of the night, and we could hardly see anything due to the lack of streetlights. There was a palpably different feel about Addis Ababa, one we sensed even while traveling the streets in George's van.

Arriving inconveniently in the wee hours of the morning, we appreciated Margaret Owen, the guest house manager, waiting up for us and showing us our apartment in the SIL guest house. I will never forget her admonition not to intake even one drop of water, not in the shower nor while brushing teeth, as it could contain bacteria that might give us diarrhea, dysentery, or worse.

My thoughts raced back to the mental wrestling match I had just had with Satan an hour before. Oh, dear, what have I gotten my family into? Will it be possible for us to survive in Africa? I had never previously considered the fact that one drop of water might do us in.

Over the next few days we focused on becoming oriented to Addis Ababa and the SIL compound and meeting many of the SIL Ethiopia branch members. However, our field training beckoned us. We found a safe place to stash all our stuff that we wouldn't need until we returned to Ethiopia, and we flew to Nairobi, Kenya, to begin "Safari."

Safari is a romantic sounding name for what used to be known as "jungle camp." I had somewhat resisted participating in Safari, arguing that I was going to be serving as an administrator in a city of nearly four million people. In addition, the language Peggy and I needed to learn was Amharic, not the Swahili taught on Safari. Why should we spend nearly three months living in a tent in rural Tanzania learning Swahili and living off the land when little of it would be relevant to our upcoming Ethiopian experience? But the "old-timers" who felt "if we had to endure jungle camp, everyone should go through jungle camp" won out, and we submitted.

That was the first year the East African Safari was to be conducted in Tanzania. All previous Safaris had been held entirely in Kenya. Our group initially met in Nairobi, Kenya, for introductions and orientation to our upcoming experience. The proclaimed objective of Safari was to "learn to love and to live in Africa." However, they couldn't disguise its real purpose as a missionary boot camp. All of us participants were to be tested regarding our survival skills in the remote wilderness of southern Tanzania.

We lived for three months with no electricity or any other modern conveniences, including e-mail and the Internet. Of course, we prepared our own food. If we got sick or hurt, the nearest hospital was hours away by minivan taxi in Tanzania's capital, Dar es Salaam.

Upon arrival at Masumbo Camp we team members were issued a tent, which we were instructed to set up under a banda—a Swahili word for the thatched-roof shelter made of bamboo. The banda offered us a little more protection from the weather and wild animals than just a tent itself. The leaders decided to allow Sam, at age twelve, to have his own tent and banda, which gave him a feeling of independence and a sense of responsibility.

We washed our clothes by hand and hung them on clothes-lines stretched between trees and poles for drying. Two long-drop outhouses, as well as a shower, stood somewhat apart from the concentration of tents. The shower setup impressed me with the ingenuity used to bring warm running water to us. The Little Ruaha River flowed down and around Masumbo Camp. The owner of the campground had dug a trench from the river at a point above the camp and channeled a small stream of water down to a big tank on the hillside above us. At a set time each afternoon a camp worker climbed the hill and lit a fire under the tank to heat the water. This gave us warm water for showers, a basic necessity of life in my opinion. Although I have always been a morning shower-taker, I gladly switched to late afternoons, after the fire had warmed the water.

In the beginning our days followed a somewhat predictable pattern. Each member of our group served on a crew of four persons for meal preparation and cleanup. Every day a crew began breakfast preparations at 5:30. Following morning devotions, team members gave presentations to the entire group, telling about various African foods and how to prepare them or some other survival topic. The remainder of our mornings we spent in class until the time came for another crew to prepare lunch. In the afternoon we attended more classes but concentrated on learning Swahili—the trade language of Tanzania, Kenya, Uganda, and other East African countries.

Beginning with our arrival at Masumbo Camp, we anticipated with some apprehension the two terms of ten days each when we would be required to live with a Tanzanian family, right in their homes. Swahili was going to be our lifeline.

Our leaders warned us, "If you can't tell your host family what you need and something about yourselves, you will have a very miserable time."

I love learning languages. This is one of the things that originally piqued my interest in Wycliffe. Swahili is one of the easiest languages in the world to learn, and I enjoyed studying this popular African language. Sam and Peggy, well, they tolerated the classes, but if they could find an excuse to volunteer for something else, they usually did.

Here's a quick Swahili aside. The Disney movie The Lion King contains several Swahili words as names for its characters. Simba, the main character's name, means "lion." Twiga means "giraffe." Rafiki means "friend," and the title of the popular song "Hakuna Matata" means "There are no worries" or "No problem!"

In the evening we studied or wrote letters. Since we were so near the equator, the sun rose at 6:30 a.m. and set at 6:30 p.m. Without electricity, there weren't a lot of choices for activities after dark. We often found ourselves getting ready for bed around 8:00 p.m. Artificial light brought mosquitoes and other wild African flying creatures, so we used our flashlights sparingly. After Peggy and I zipped ourselves in our tent at night, we always completed the ritual of lighting up our tents with our flashlights and killing all the mosquitoes that had entered during the day. Mosquitoes, in addition to being terribly annoying throughout the night, can carry malaria.

At first we worried about Sam over there in his tent all alone, but soon we realized he really liked it. Our British tent neighbors in another direction, Jonathan and Jayne Price, had two small daughters. Their malaria prophylaxis medicine caused horrible nightmares. Those two poor little girls woke in the middle of the night (waking us also, as there isn't much sound insulation with tents) screaming about snakes and dragons and spiders and everything else scary. This happened nearly every night.

Coincidentally, we found ourselves on Safari with a woman, Keri, who had been in our Quest class twelve years before. Keri and I served on the same kitchen crew. (The crew consisted of Gary, Keri, Jeri, and Roland. Instead of Roland we felt we should have had a Larry or a Mary.) She and I had a secret greeting each morning as we whispered to each other, "Forty-two days left," "Only twenty-five days left," etc. I guess we thought that greeting served to convince ourselves that someday Safari would be over.

Peggy and I survived Safari by always being the first to volunteer for anything. In the U.S. Army volunteering for a task was usually a silly thing to do. On Safari volunteering brought opportunities and a welcome break from the drudgery of camp. Our volunteering got us to a village church one Sunday, to a town church another Sunday, to market to purchase food supplies, and to a prehistoric archeological site that still had stone tools lying around on the ground.

One of the requirements of Safari was to live with a Tanzanian family in the nearby town of Iringa for ten days. Eventually the day arrived that our leaders took us to a church in Iringa where we each met our host family. Peggy, Sam, and I were assigned to a family headed by an accountant for the phone company. Our hosts' names were Philip and Grace Mseya. They lived in an extremely small house. And typical of many African families, in addition to the father, mother, and two sons, several other relatives and friends lived in little nooks and crannies of their "courtyard."

The Mseyas planned for Peggy and me to have a tiny bedroom with a bed and mattress about the size of a full-size bed, while Sam was to sleep on a sofa in the living room. However, the first afternoon, as we visited in that tiny living room, Peggy saw a rat scurry up the wall into the space above the ceiling directly over Sam's bed. Peggy insisted to our hostess that Sam, instead, sleep with us.

The mattress on our bed was actually wider than the bed frame, so the mattress curved up and over the frame on the side nearest the wall. The sleeping arrangement was Peggy scrunched in the middle between Sam and me, Sam on the high part of the bed against the wall, always rolling down into Peggy, and me on the outside edge, nearly falling out. For those ten nights, we also struggled with trying to keep our mosquito net somewhat intact around our bed, hoping to keep those annoying and dangerous pests away from us.

We didn't have a lot to do during the days, so Stanley, one of the residents at our house, showed us around the town. Stanley was college age, so the Tanzanians in the town who became our good friends were almost all in their twenties. But they were very friendly and helpful to us, and through them we got to know Iringa very well. We found the one shop in town that sold candy, cookies, potato chips, and other snacks. If we could find any occasion to slip away from our host family or to pass by this shop, we ran in and purchased what snacks we could, given our limited time and Tanzanian shillings.

Our stay in Iringa was made more tolerable as a result of an occasion that took place a couple of weeks before, when the leaders of Safari asked for volunteers. Peggy and I, as usual, stepped forward immediately. That volunteer opportunity resulted in our going to the Anglican church in town, with its very liturgical style of worship. Our Apostolic Christian worship style does not include this kind of liturgy, so we found ourselves in a quite unfamiliar church setting. But it was an escape from

Masumbo Camp, and we rejoiced in joining our Tanzanian brothers and sisters in worshipping Jesus.

At that church we met a young missionary couple, Rich and Lisa Hensey, who taught at a local college. Lisa was from Clinton, Illinois, which is only about twenty miles (thirty kilometers) from our hometown of Bloomington. We had a nice visit with them, and they invited us to come to their house sometime. Rich and Lisa felt compassion for us when they heard about our living conditions in camp. Knowing we would someday soon be staying with a Tanzanian family in their town, I asked them to draw a map to their house.

That map, along with their telephone number, was a lifesaver for us. Toward the end of our ten days of town living we called the Henseys, asking if we could visit them. They warmly welcomed us, so we took a minivan taxi to their house. We basked in the luxury of their house outfitted with sit-down ceramic toilets, soft chairs, a computer, and warm running water on demand. However, they had another appointment which cut our visit short for that day. They invited us to come back again the following day.

Our Tanzanian host family always watched us very closely. We weren't sure whether it was because the Mseyas were concerned for our safety, didn't want to share us with anybody else, were instructed not to let us out of their sight by our leaders, or for some other reason. But we found it nearly impossible to ever escape their clutches, leaving us even more desirous of independence and freedom.

We pretty much had gone "AWOL" (Absent Without Leave) from our host family when we went to Rich and Lisa's house the first time. Since we were desperate to experience life outside the cramped confines of our hosts' itty-bitty house, we were willing to take the risk to escape again. Therefore, we told the Henseys we would love to return the next day, even though it meant we would again have to stealthily escape from our hosts' eyesight. We also asked if it would be possible to send an e-mail to our family members back in the States, telling them they could e-mail or call us the next day at 4:00 p.m. Tanzania time. They said it would be fine, and we sent our families the e-mail address and telephone number where they could contact us.

During our taxi ride back to the Mseyas' house we began to worry about how we would ever again break free to get back to the Henseys the next day. We couldn't tell them we would be receiving telephone calls, because they would wonder why we didn't give our family members their telephone number to call. They didn't have a computer, and we could tell they did not understand computers or e-mail. So we told our host family we needed to go across town the next day to receive an e-mail at 4:00. As everyone who has used e-mail knows, e-mails can come at any time and they stay in the inbox until they are read, perhaps hours or days later.

Our excuse seemed to work, although our hosts felt like they should come along with us. We assured them we would be safe and fine and would come right back.

We took the minivan taxi to the Henseys' house. They excitedly told us we had received an e-mail from my mom and dad, which they had printed off for us. Then we waited with anticipation to see if there would be any phone calls. The phone rang, and it was Peggy's mom. She shared a lot of news. She was worried whether we were safe and whether we had enough food to eat. We happily assured her we were okay on both accounts.

Peggy hung up from talking with her, and Becky called. When Becky finished, Angie called. We didn't realize it, but they had made out among themselves a calling schedule so they would not be competing for time slots. We loved hearing from them and finding out all the happenings back home in the States, in our family circle, and out in the rest of the world.

After the e-mail and phone calls, we enjoyed a wonderful shower and felt really clean for the first time in two months. I shaved with a real mirror and without being rushed. We exulted in the luxuries of the Western life until it was time to go. Peggy, Sam, and I said our good-byes and thank-yous and told Rich and Lisa from the bottom of our hearts that they would never know how encouraging and meaningful their hospitality was to us. That luxurious experience sustained us through the remainder of our ten days in Iringa.

One of the many experiences I will never forget from our town living experience occurred with our shower facilities. The Mseyas cleaned up a tiny storage room for showering. It had a cement floor, dirty, but at least we had a solid place to stand. They hung a sheet of plastic tarp over the opening and gave us a couple of hoe handles to place against the outside of the tarp to keep the wind from blowing it open. The ladies of the house heated water over the fire for us and put it in a dishpan. We took the warm water into the little room and "showered" by soaping up and pouring the water over ourselves with a pitcher.

One day I heard a shriek from that room while Peggy was bathing. The wind had blown the hoe handles down, and the tarp was waving in the wind, with Peggy in her birthday suit exposed to the outside. I had to quickly run and put the tarp back in place and properly position the hoe handles for her to finish her bath and save her dignity.

Eventually the day came to give the family members and the others living in the compound their gifts and say our good-byes. After leaving their home we took a minivan to the bus station, found the bus to Masumbo Camp, and returned "home." We enjoyed seeing our fellow Safari members again and sharing stories. Almost all had had experiences like ours, which also made them anxious to return to camp. One family told a real horror story of how they were pretty much subjected to slave labor, required to work in the fields and babysit so their hosts could go out on the town and visit their friends. It could have been much worse for us, we found out.

Our village living experience was scheduled for one week after we returned from town living. We thought, "Man, if living in town with a family for ten days was that difficult, how will we ever survive the village?"

The fateful departure day arrived, and a small group of us Safari participants boarded the Land Rover along with our basic supplies for the next week and a half. After about two hours on very rough roads and getting lost multiple times, we found the host family home for Jonathan and Jayne Price and their daughters and dropped them off. Our Safari leader told the Prices, since they were so remote and no bus passed through that village, he would be back to pick them up on the appointed day to return to camp. This turned out to be significant for us, too.

We drove down endless rutted roads until we got to another village where two single guys would stay. Those two men didn't want us to leave them behind. Their host was a farmer, and they had visions of hoeing corn by hand for ten days.

Eventually, after more and more driving and to a point I had no idea where we were or where Iringa was, they dropped Peggy, Sam, and me off with our host family, the Mhangas. Our Safari leader explained to the host family what was expected of each party and prayed with all of us before he left. He also admonished us that exactly ten days from that day we had to be back in Masumbo Camp, having been resourceful enough to find our own way back.

The Mhanga family consisted of a mother, father, two daughters, and a son. They gave us a bedroom, which we found to be larger and nicer than in town, and this time we had two beds—one larger one for Peggy and me and a twin-size bed for Sam. As usual, several other relatives and friends lived in and around the host family's compound.

The entire family welcomed us with friendly smiles and seemed as nervous to have us living with them as we were nervous about being there. The two girls seemed particularly curious to see us, and we were excited to hear them speak a little English. They wanted to tell us everything in a combination of English and Swahili, and their excitement showed as they led us around their farm and small village.

When I saw the outhouse located a long way from the living quarters, maybe half the length of a football field, I wondered how I would do with my usual need to use the bathroom in the middle of the night. I could just step outside the house door and pee, but would that be the proper thing to do? Or should I shuffle through the rocks and grass over to the outhouse, risking finding snakes, hyenas, or other African creatures getting there and back? And besides that, the choo (Swahili for outhouse) was only one step above being in the open anyway. I ended up doing the right thing, taking my flashlight and swishing my way through the grass to warn rodents, snakes, and hyenas that I was coming, and used the outhouse as any civilized man would.

Our first night there a group of singers from their church (Lulanzi Lutheran Church—Lulanzi was the name of the village) came and sang for us. Our host family, the Mhangas, took their three nicest chairs outside into the courtyard for Peggy, Sam, and me to sit on for the upcoming ceremony. Soon, more and more people came and welcomed us. As we saw their outpouring of praise, our hearts were deeply touched. The ambience of this home and surrounding village was much more accommodating than town living had been.

For us this village was precipitously close to the edge of the earth. No white person had ever stayed in Lulanzi before. Many children saw the first white person of their lives when they saw Sam, Peggy, or me. We have many unfortunate memories of walking along the paths and encountering a little kid who would run, screaming at the top of his lungs for his mommy. He had just seen the ugliest, most disgusting creature of his life.

There were two vehicles in Lulanzi. A college-educated agriculturist had a motorcycle, and a businessman had a truck used to haul cabbages to Iringa on certain days of the week. But our hosts assured us that a bus passed through Lulanzi every morning and that would be our transportation back to Iringa and on to Masumbo Camp on the designated day.

Our host family treated us to the best of their ability and with the greatest hospitality. The entire populace of the village soon knew of our presence, and the people always greeted and welcomed us as we walked the paths that crisscrossed the village.

At church on Sunday our host and the other leaders put the three of us up in front of the whole congregation. Mr. Mhanga was an M'zee, a Swahili word meaning one of the respected elders of the community. He asked me to preach in church while his daughter, Shani, translated. Despite my concerns about preaching, I submitted to his request. Since we were in lion country I knew my audience understood lions. So my sermon was on "Daniel and the Lion's Den." Due to my translator's limited English and my limited Swahili, I kept the message simple.

In rural African culture, supper is always eaten very late, usually around 9:30 or 10:00 at night. Peggy, Sam, and I always felt dreadfully tired by the time supper rolled around, and we would have preferred just to go to bed. But, of course, that would have been entirely culturally inappropriate behavior on our part. The women work either in the fields or at some other job in the village—perhaps as a shopkeeper or at the grinding mill. By the time they get home, capture and kill the chicken, peel the potatoes, grind the corn, get the fire going, and boil the water, along with all the other preparations, it is 9:00 before any food can possibly be served.

The only electricity in Lulanzi was in the batteries of flashlights and tape players. There were certainly no microwave ovens or food processors there. Life was basic, and cooking had to be done over a wood or charcoal fire.

The ladies always ate in the smoke-filled outdoor kitchen. In spite of their culture, they always wanted Peggy to eat inside the house with the men. Sometimes Peggy insisted on staying outside with them. Our kind hosts never wanted us to do any work, so we had to either beg to help or just barge our way in. Some ways we were able to help were with their water collection, water conservation, and bathing.

Right away we noticed the Mhangas were very conservative with water. Not a drop of water was spilled or used foolishly. However, they always boiled about three or four liters (around a gallon) of water for me each morning to take a warm shower. The shower stall was outside, maybe 100 feet (30 meters) from the house, and consisted of a grass and cornstalk fence. Inside was a dirt floor with a rock in the middle to stand on. Grass and cornstalks don't make an impervious fence, so I tried to take my shower very early in the morning to avoid as many voyeurs as possible. (I guess the little kids were curious about what a white man looked like underneath his clothes.) And, as soon as I stepped off the rock, my feet sunk into mud, which sort of negated the purpose of the shower (at least for my feet).

Not knowing what kind of showers we might find in Africa, we had brought a solar shower with us from the States. It was a rugged plastic bag with a short hose on the bottom that terminated in a small showerhead. A spigot controlled the water flow. Once filled with water, the bag is left in the sun during the day to warm. In the evening the bag, now full of warm water, is hung up and used for a refreshing warm shower. However, since the ladies of the household always heated water for me over the fire in the mornings, I didn't have to heat the solar shower water in the sun.

Every morning I poured the warm water they prepared for me into the solar shower, hung it on a tree limb, and had my bath, feeling somewhat exposed to the neighborhood by the cornstalk curtain. The cool morning air caused steam to rise from my body.

In addition to being conservative with water, I also noticed when it rained our hosts collected all the water possible from the roofs. One day as the girls went to fetch water Sam and I asked to go along and help. At first they refused, but eventually they relented and allowed us to tag along. Sam and I each took a jerry can and set off with the girls. It seemed that the boys and men never helped with this task. We walked and walked down the road, possibly a mile. Then we descended a long steep hill. I began to worry about how I would carry five gallons (twenty liters) of water all the way back to the farmhouse. I felt humbled as I discovered the extreme effort these girls exerted each day to make water available for us.

At the bottom of the hill, sticking out of the rocks was a pipe with spring water constantly flowing from it. We all filled our jerry cans and began the arduous trek back up the hill and up the long road home. Sam and I arrived back at our hosts' house with tired, aching muscles, glad the job was over. With this new knowledge, I vowed I could take a shower with just one liter (one quart) of water. And from that day forward, I did. If the ladies heated three or four liters of water for me, I left two or three liters of water in the solar shower bag. However, I noticed that by the next morning it was always empty. I guessed that some host family members were using my leftover water for their own showers. Therefore, when we left I gave them the solar shower as a gift. The family was elated, and I knew they would make good use of it.

As our time in Lulanzi drew to an end, we made arrangements to take the public bus back to Iringa as instructed by our Safari leaders. On our last evening in the village our hosts again took their three best chairs out into the dirt courtyard. Other villagers began to arrive, and the Mhangas asked Peggy, Sam, and me to sit on the three chairs. The choir that had greeted us our first evening serenaded us again with hymns. More and more people showed up. Soon the courtyard was completely packed, but more guests continued to arrive. Little children were not allowed in, so they gawked through holes in the fence. To the beat of a large drum the townsfolk started dancing in a big circle and requested that we join them.

We believe nearly the entire village turned out to say good-bye to us. The significance and sincerity of this farewell party touched our hearts deeply. Without being able to speak our language, they told us we belonged to them and were welcome back in their village any time.

Partway through that Sunday evening ceremony, M'zee Mhanga called me to go inside the house with him. He had a grave look on his face as he told me, "The public bus is in Iringa for servicing. It won't come through here until Tuesday morning. I know you need to be back to camp tomorrow. I'm very sorry about this. I have tried to talk the cabbage truck driver into taking your family, but he has refused."

"Please, M'zee, try to convince the cabbage truck driver to take us. It's the only possibility for us to get to Iringa tomorrow. We'll ride on top of the cabbages, if necessary."

M'zee went out into the night to again talk to the cabbage truck driver. He returned with the good news. "I've convinced him to take your family to Iringa. He wants you to be at the side of the road in front of our house at 4:30 tomorrow morning."

"No problem; we'll be there. Thank you so much for arranging this."

We rejoined the party outside and had a long time of saying farewells and giving hugs and expressing hope that someday we would return. If we ever will get back to Lulanzi, God only knows. Regardless, we will sit around majestic tables in heaven with the Lulanzi Christians someday.

We packed our bags and set our alarm for 4:00 a.m. Even though we eagerly anticipated getting back to our Safari team, we felt no desperation to do so this time around.

That morning the three of us were just preparing to go out

to stand by the road when we heard the cabbage truck accelerate past our house about fifteen minutes early, not even slowing a little bit.

We were shell-shocked. Our only hope for getting to Iringa had just raced by, reneging on his promise to pick us up. What could we do? As we discussed our plight with M'zee, I told him, "You know, M'zee, I heard the Safari leader tell the Price family he would be by to pick them up today, since there is no public transportation from their village. Is there any way we could get a message over to them asking the Land Rover driver to come and pick us up as well?"

The M'zee thought over this a bit and responded, "My nephew could ride his bicycle over there. It would take about two hours. But if he left right now he could probably make it before the Land Rover got there."

"Could you please ask your nephew to try?"

At that time the sky was still pitch black, and it was impossible to see the road. M'zee woke his nephew and sent him off on the long and dangerous bicycle ride.

We never heard back from the nephew, although we will be forever grateful for his sacrificial help for us. It turned out he saw the Land Rover on the road near the other village and told our Safari leader about our plight. Just as with the Price family, we had no transportation available to us, and would he come and pick us up too?

Without the availability of telephone communication we didn't know until later that day, when the Land Rover showed up at the house, that the connection had been made. Through the resourcefulness and sacrificial assistance of others we passed the test and made it back to camp on time.

Our family had many pleasant and interesting experiences in Lulanzi. Even though we had dreaded spending our time there because of our town living experience, it turned out to be just the opposite. It may have been the most remote place we had ever been on earth. Even though we were separated by languages and cultures that were miles apart and even though we had no telephone, electricity, running water, Internet, or taxis, we found friends filled with happiness and contentment and loving Jesus in a genuine way. They demonstrated that love of Jesus to us—we being the strangers they took in to their own homes. We still keep in touch with the Mhanga family from Lulanzi, as well as the Mseya family from Iringa.

CHAPTER 18

Back to Ethiopia

Safari at Masumbo Camp reminded me of my experience in the U.S. Army. I had been drafted into the army during the Vietnam War from 1970-1972. At that time many of us veterans said we wouldn't trade anything for our experiences, but you couldn't pay us a million dollars to do it again.

"All good things must come to an end," the saying goes, and Safari was no exception. Our group went to the Indian Ocean coast of Tanzania to the town of Bagamoya for a debriefing. Despite the natural beauty and relaxation we enjoyed there, Peggy, Sam, and I were really ready to get back to Ethiopia. After debriefing we boarded a bus for a fifteen-hour ride (in one stretch!) back to Nairobi, Kenya.

When we arrived in Nairobi, Peggy and I received a message informing us that the SIL branch in Ethiopia was having its annual conference, leaving no guest house rooms available for us. They asked if we could find something to do in Kenya for about three or four days and delay our flight back to Addis Ababa.

Even though we had just spent nearly three months in the remote interior of Africa, we realized we knew nothing about Nairobi or Kenya, except what little we picked up as we passed through the first time on our way to Tanzania. The request for us to entertain ourselves in Kenya for four days surprised us. In a turn of fate that turned out to be prescient three years later, the Spirit prompted us to call our friends Mark and Pam Hodel.

Missionaries on the staff of Rift Valley Academy (RVA) in Kijabe, Kenya, Mark and Pam served with AIM (Africa Inland Mission). They grew up in the same denomination we did, so we knew not only them but some of their family members also.

Kijabe is located about an hour outside Nairobi. A Christian school, composed of kindergarten through twelfth grade, RVA provides an excellent education for children whose parents are missionaries in Africa. Most of the students board there, even the little tykes.

After we told Mark and Pam our situation, they graciously invited us to go out to Kijabe and stay with them during our "exile" from returning to Ethiopia. We had a great time with them at Kijabe, sharing experiences and soaking up all the advice we could glean from them regarding life in Africa and life as missionaries.

The most surprising event of our trip to RVA occurred as we prepared to leave. Sam, to this point in his life, had never expressed any feelings or opinions regarding his education. Seven years at little Towanda Elementary School in Illinois, home-schooled by his parents, enrolled for one semester of seventh grade at huge Duncanville (Texas) Junior High School, home-schooled by two Kenyan girls on Safari—he took it all in stride. But, as we said our good-byes at RVA, Sam made his first-ever request regarding his education.

"Mom and Dad, you go on back to Ethiopia. I want to stay here and go to school," he proposed.

Getting admitted to RVA is very difficult. Some missionary parents put their child on the waiting list while they are still expecting the baby. Besides that, one condition we had placed before the Lord in our search for a country to serve in was that Sam could live at home with us and not have to attend a boarding school in another country.

Because of the fact he could not simply enroll and begin school at RVA at that time, Sam joined Peggy and me as the three of us packed and departed for Ethiopia. Little did we know, though, how prophetic Sam's words would be a short stretch down the road!

We flew back to Ethiopia and arrived at the SIL branch on the afternoon of the last day of the conference. We joined them for the wrapping-up activities and were able to meet many of the members of the branch.

CHAPTER 19

SIL Branch, Addis Ababa, Ethiopia

Around lunchtime on Sam's very first day of school at Bingham Academy in Addis Ababa, Peggy received a call from the school office. "Please come as quickly as you can to pick up Sam. School is being dismissed early."

"What in the world is going on?" she asked herself.

Peggy and several other SIL moms raced to the school to find that some Addis Ababa University students had rioted. The university students' rioting attracted some high school students to join them. In addition, street kids who had nothing better to do and were always looking for some excitement participated. They went on a rampage, throwing rocks and mobbing the shopping area called Piassa, destroying signs, breaking windows, and looting the stores.

The police and soldiers responded by beating the students and firing shots, creating mayhem. Not knowing how severe the riots might become, Sam's school ordered all the students to go home and announced there would be no school for the next day at least.

Finding a way to the school and back home again proved very difficult for Peggy and the others. The police and soldiers blocked the streets and took control. Essentially the town was under martial law. Sam, though, thought it was pretty cool that on his first day of school in Ethiopia classes were called off early due to rioting.

We also officially began our SIL office duties on that Monday of the riots.

The focus of this book is to document how God took an Illinois farm boy (and his wife) and worked in his life to become a missionary in Africa with a variety of experiences and responsibilities that no one could ever have predicted. Our two and a half years with the SIL branch in Ethiopia consisted of many amazing (and mundane) experiences, tests, and relationships, which could be the subject of another book. However, I feel compelled to include some stories and experiences that took place during our service at the Ethiopia SIL branch that are central to my missionary journey and the Lord's directing that journey from above.

Although Ethiopia has upwards of ninety languages and people groups, Amharic is the "national" language—the language of education, government, and commerce. Therefore, learning Amharic became our first assignment. Even though there are many languages in Ethiopia, only a handful have had their alphabets developed and some portion of the Bible translated for the people who speak those languages. That, of course, is the reason Wycliffe Bible Translators is there.

I have dabbled in several languages—Latin, German (at one time I was nearly fluent), Russian, French, Portuguese, Swahili—and far and away the most difficult is Amharic. Many Europeans who know four or five languages come to Ethiopia expecting to simply add another language to their repertoire. Some do learn Amharic; however, most burn out before they gain any proficiency.

Amharic is a Semitic language closely related to Hebrew and Arabic. It has its own alphabet, consisting of nearly 300 characters. The construction of the language is completely different from the "European" languages I had previously studied. One has to twist his brain around in a different way to understand and to speak Amharic.

Here is a sample of Amharic: ፍቅር የሌለው· እግዚአብሔርን አያውቅም፤ እግዚአብሔር ፍቅር ነውና (1ኛ የሐንስ 4:8).

It says in English: "Whoever does not love does not know God, because God is love" (1 John 4:8 NIV).

During Amharic language school, I worked part-time as SIL's director of administration. At the conclusion of school I started working full-time, on a lateral level with the director of language programs. Both of us directors reported to the overall director of the branch. The director of language programs oversaw all the exciting disciplines of translation, literacy, and Scripture use. I was responsible for the boring stuff—finances, human resources, information technology, grounds and facilities, etc.

Peggy had two jobs. The first, guest house manager, involved the difficult task of ensuring that everyone who wanted to stay in our guest house was able to do so. This responsibility included supervising the guest house workers. The position of member services manager, her second job, necessitated her handling all kinds of requests from SIL members, such as visas, airline tickets, work permits, residence IDs, and personal purchases.

As Dan Butler, Africa area director, had told us in Dallas, the greatest need for administrative help in Africa was in Ethiopia. Administratively, I found the branch to be in somewhat of a mess when I first assumed my position. There was no wage scale for the workers, no uniform way of administering salary increases and promotions, no effective employee manual, no organization chart, and no insurance program for the cars, buildings, and workers' compensation. The lack of insurance was incomprehensible for a former State Farm Insurance employee. My past experience with corporate budgets also proved to be useful. I was soon convinced that Dan Butler was right on target with his assessment of the situation of the management needs of the Ethiopian SIL branch and that my training and experience would be helpful.

Bible translators, like artists, are creative and "right-brained."

Most of the foreign administrative staff either were former translators or performed both translation and administrative duties simul-
taneously. Therefore, a lot of the organizational, administrative,
and analytical aspects of running a business had been neglected.

Eventually, as I got those administrative projects under control, the work turned into a job similar to my experience at State
Farm: get up, go to work, handle the problems and the responsibilities of the day, go home, and get up the next day and do the
same thing over again.

Without our being aware of it at the time, God began putting
the pieces into place for the next task He had lined up for us.

I have kept a detailed daily journal ever since we moved to
Africa. As I reread it in preparation for writing this book, amazing
revelations jumped out at me. Looking back with twenty-twenty
hindsight, and knowing how our two and a half years at SIL
ended, I realize how very clearly my journal foreshadowed our
missionary career change. However, at that time, not knowing
God's plan for our lives, I only experienced what seemed to be one
frustrating situation after another.

At the branch conference that had been held at the end of our
Safari training (and had delayed our return to Addis Ababa
because of lack of guest house space), the SIL members held elections for branch officer positions. Mary Breeze, the director who
had graciously invited us to come to Ethiopia, was replaced by a
member of the branch who was translating the New Testament
for the Basketto people group. The new director was British, as
Mary also was.

Problems began to develop in the relationship between the
new SIL director, along with his wife, and Peggy and me. The first
occurred in September 2002. We had been in Africa, at that point,
one year and nine months.

Wycliffe's furlough policy entitled a member to one year of
furlough after four years overseas or, in place of that, six months of

furlough after two years. When we arrived at the Ethiopia SIL branch we asked Mary Breeze for an exception to this policy. Instead of taking large chunks of furlough, such as one year or six months, we asked to take five or six weeks of vacation each year. Mary agreed to that arrangement. Even in spite of this agreement, by the following summer of 2003 we would have been on the overseas mission field with Wycliffe for two and a half years, easily long enough to qualify for six months furlough.

This arrangement was important to us because our two daughters lived back in the States, we had aging parents, and we had a church family and many friends we wanted to see more often than simply every other year or every four years. In addition, we had the following things to consider regarding furlough: who would do our jobs when we were gone for six months or more, what we would do with our house during that long time, what we would do with our car, and what we would do with our house worker and guards. Taking just a few weeks of vacation each year seemed like a lot better option for both SIL and us, even though in the long run it meant a lot less time off for us.

When we asked for approximately six weeks off during the following summer of 2003 we received a great deal of resistance from the director. If we had asked the Wycliffe U.S. office for six months furlough, it would have been readily granted. And this option tempted us. But we preferred to visit our American home for only a short time and quickly return to our responsibilities in Ethiopia.

The director and his wife had come to Ethiopia as Bible translators several years before. He was an example of a Bible translator who moved in from the field to take an administrative post in the branch headquarters.

I assured the director I had experienced my share of administrative headaches at State Farm and I had no desire to become the head of the branch. Very content to be "No. 2," I told him I never intended to run against him in any elections for branch director.

As the branch improved administratively and the SIL members realized there was someone in the director of administration position who got things done, who could make decisions, and who wanted to serve them, they increasingly came to me with their issues rather than to the director. To stem this tide, the director issued directives stating that only he was authorized to make certain kinds of decisions. I cringed when people continued to come to me regarding the "forbidden" issues and I had to tell them to see the director. They didn't want to go to him, and I felt bad sending them to him.

Some time after his election to the director position, the then-personnel manager, Hilleen Middleton (who also helped us make the decision to serve in Ethiopia) moved with her husband, Mike, and their children to the U.S. The Middletons had helped us in many other ways, including hosting us for several days in their home when we first arrived in Ethiopia. And Sam developed a very close friendship with their son, Kevin.

To fill the empty position, the director appointed his wife as the new personnel manager in place of Hilleen. This consolidated within his family two very powerful positions in the branch office. With his wife serving as personnel manager, they knew all details of each member's life.

My journal entries from that time period clearly describe the downward-spiraling relationship between the director and his wife and me. I am reminded of tension at daily prayer meetings when they were present. I especially remember them purposely boycotting a branch-wide prayer meeting when Peggy and I led it. I am reminded of countless times when the director called me into his office to reprimand me for one of my decisions or because of the occurrence of certain events. I have never apologized so many times in my life as I did during those months leading up to our departure from SIL. Whenever I was called to his office, I simply prepared myself to say "I'm sorry." Regardless of how much I informed him of my decisions or counseled with him before taking any action, he seemed to find ways to criticize my work.

The director micromanaged my position and continually checked to see who was in my office asking for advice or help rather than going to him. I assured him over and over that I had no designs on the director position and I felt very content letting him be the director.

He displayed his unsubstantiated concerns at the branch conference when the elections for the executive committee (EC) took place. The EC is the board of directors of the branch. During the session of taking names for nominations to the EC, someone nominated me first. The director jumped up and said he didn't think it would be good for someone from administration to be on the EC and that my name should be stricken. There was no such rule or bylaw.

One day a very angry SIL missionary from Finland burst into my office. She had been home in Finland for a long furlough and had just returned to Ethiopia. When she left for Finland, before Peggy and I even arrived in Ethiopia, she asked the then member services manager to take insurance coverage off her car. She planned to park the vehicle in the SIL compound during her absence. When she returned from her furlough, she found the insurance had not been removed and she had been charged for coverage each month while she was absent.

First she questioned her boss, the language programs director, who supervised all personnel working directly on translation, literacy, and Scripture use. He referred her to me. Not only was she very upset, but she also demanded SIL refund her all the money she had paid for car insurance during her absence.

I looked into the situation and verified that she had received monthly financial statements from our branch that clearly listed insurance as one of the deductions from her monthly income. She had ample time and many reminders to let the branch know the insurance had not been removed as she requested.

Since the director was micromanaging me, I discussed the issue with him. He looked it all over and agreed she should have read her statements and contacted us regarding the mistake. When I relayed this decision back to her, she stormed over to the director's office. He caved and wrote me up for not being culturally sensitive. I still don't see how cultural sensitivity fit into that scenario, as it seemed to have been the way the matter should be handled regardless if the person were Finnish, American, or British.

In the fall of 2002, we American members of the branch decided to continue the tradition of preparing a large Thanksgiving feast for all members of the branch, regardless of nationality. Peggy and I volunteered to coordinate the meal and accompanying program. All members fondly remembered Thanksgiving meals from years past and looked forward to sharing this celebration with us Americans again.

Peggy, the consummate hostess, does a great job of preparing and serving meals. She put her whole heart into this Thanksgiving celebration. Since not many turkeys are raised in Ethiopia, turkey meat must be imported and is very expensive. But Peggy didn't waver in her determination to serve turkey. She found imported turkeys, each one costing $50 U.S. We Americans took a collection and forked over $100 for two small turkeys. Others contributed cranberry sauce and bought pumpkins. Peggy put together the typical American Thanksgiving feast, eagerly anticipated by all.

When we were all seated at our Pilgrim-and-turkey decorated tables, I opened with a prayer and following that read President George W. Bush's 2002 Thanksgiving Day proclamation. I read it word for word with no explanatory remarks other than to say I chose to read it in case members from other countries wanted to know a little more about the background of this great American holiday.

No one said anything to Peggy or me at that time, except to express deep thanks and appreciation for inviting them and sharing our holiday. However, months later at my performance review, the director wrote the following verbatim assessment:

> Gary relates well to Ethiopians and has made excellent progress in language learning. However he can come across as American-centric to his European colleagues. He needs to recognise [British spelling] the international nature of SIL and develop sensitivity towards those of other nationalities. He was surprised to learn that some felt awkward when he read out the US Presidential speech thanking God for the blessings of being American, at the SIL thanksgiving-day [sic] meal open to all members.

I was the most surprised person in Ethiopia that day. I wondered if we should have restricted attendance to Americans only. Regardless, if we had been invited to a British celebration, I would have felt it more than appropriate to hear the queen's comments. And I doubt I would have expressed any lack of cultural sensitivity on the part of the person who had invited me.

Without unnecessarily belaboring this strained relationship with additional examples, I believe one more incident explains a lot. The situation involved two American Wycliffe couples—Marvin and Suzanne Beachy, who were translating the Bible for the Diizi tribe in remote southwestern Ethiopia, and Randall and Melanie Lemley, who served in SIL branch administration. Marvin and Randall drove to the Beachys' Diizi home, a trip that usually required at least two hard days to travel one way. On their return to Addis Ababa Randall was driving, and in order to avoid something on the road he got too close to the edge and rolled the vehicle a couple of times. It came to rest on its roof.

In what can only be described as a miracle, no one was seriously hurt, including the Ethiopians riding with them. And in one of the best engineering and ingenuity efforts I've ever heard of, they rolled the vehicle back onto its wheels, pounded out the sheet metal of the cab, cleared the fenders from the tires, and started the engine. Unbelievably, they got that wreck moving and slowly crept to the town of Mizan Teferi.

In Mizan Teferi they found a hotel and reported to the police. Until the circumstances of the accident could be determined, the police put them under house arrest in the hotel and did not allow them to continue their journey on to Addis Ababa by public transportation. Since Ethiopian police departments have no money, they had no vehicle to go to the scene of the wreck. They needed to wait for a vehicle to come and take them to the accident site, causing a great delay for Marvin and Randall's return to their families.

As the days rolled by, Randall and Marvin's wives and children back in Addis Ababa couldn't rest because of their anxiety and concern for their husbands and fathers. Marvin and Randall regularly called me with updates on their situation. I passed the information along to their wives and also to the director. Each time they called me instead of the director, the director's anger ratcheted up another notch. I pleaded with them to please call the director, but they continued to call me. I tremblingly passed each report to the director. I tried to reassure him that I had told them to call him. But since they didn't, he refused to believe me.

After several days of this uncertainty and the stalling by the police, I called the United States Embassy to report that two American men were being held under house arrest in Mizan Teferi. The embassy officials immediately started working on the situation.

The director, for his part, called the local Mekane Yesus Church (an evangelical denomination) and asked them to go to Mizan Teferi and check out the case. And just as the house arrest situation was coming to a head, the director and the language programs director left together for a meeting outside of Addis. The director left his wife, the personnel manager, and me in charge of the crisis.

Given that arrangement, and since the director had overruled my decision to involve the U.S. Embassy, I assumed he really meant his wife was in charge. When she called me on the Sunday morning of the crisis I was quite surprised. She asked, "Gary, can you come to the office now to discuss Marvin and Randall's situation?"

"Sure, I can come. I'll be right there."

When I arrived, she explained in painstaking detail the situation, as if I had not been in the middle of it for all those days. Then she asked, "What do you think we should do?"

"Well, your husband is the director. Since he wants the Mekane Yesus Church to handle the situation, I am willing to go along with that. And because he appointed you to oversee the situation, I respect your position."

"No, no, we need to know what each other is thinking so we can act as a team. What should we do?"

"The director has made the decision. I'm willing to go along with it."

"Please tell me how you think we should proceed."

"Well, based on your husband's approach to the situation, it really would do no good for me to add my opinion."

Again she asked what I thought.

Finally, I responded, "If I were out there in Marvin and Randall's situation I would want my embassy involved. I would rather have the resources of the U.S. Embassy working for me than a church pastor."

That statement sealed my doom.

CHAPTER 20

God's Hand,
Steady at the Wheel

Project Mercy, a mission organization based in Fort Wayne, Indiana, was founded by an Ethiopian-American couple, Demeke Tekle-wold (husband) and Marta Gebre-tsadick (wife). Since their names are somewhat long and difficult for Westerners to pronounce, they generally are referred to as "Marta and Deme," as Marta is the spokesperson and visionary of the family. Deme comes along and makes sure everything gets done properly.

Marta and Deme's story and their conviction to help the people of their native Ethiopia are well documented in Marta's book Sheltered by the King (Chosen Books, 1983) and other publications. Because their story is so rich and compelling I could not possibly do it justice here. I will merely recap some of the highlights of their lives in order to provide a basic background for this segment of my missionary journey.

Marta was born to poor parents in rural Ethiopia. But Marta did not allow her humble beginnings to affect her strong desire to succeed in life. Through circumstances that could have only been coordinated by God, she caught the attention of the king of Ethiopia, Emperor Haile Selassie, at an early age. When she was fifteen, her parents arranged for her to be married to a fifty-two-year-old Norwegian missionary. Although he promised Marta an education in the United States, he didn't follow through. Finally, after

Marta had two children, her mother arranged for her to get her long-dreamed-of American education. Deme met her at college and liked her but was surprised to find she was already married.

Shortly after Marta returned to Ethiopia with her degree, her Norwegian husband died, freeing her to marry Deme. Together they had an additional two sons. Deme became a very successful trader. Marta continued to be shown great favor by Emperor Haile Selassie. He appointed her as the first female senator in Ethiopia. Later she rose to prominence in the Ministry of Foreign Affairs.

When the communists (called the Derg, which means "Committee" in Amharic) toppled and killed Emperor Haile Selassie in 1974, Marta and Deme also feared for their lives because of their high positions. When the Derg's threats against them rose to a fever pitch, they were forced to escape to Kenya with little else besides the clothes on their backs and three of their sons (the fourth was studying outside Ethiopia). Their harrowing story of escape, avoiding Derg soldiers, and facing peril as their 4WD vehicle broke down, leaving them nearly dead of thirst, hunger, and sickness, clearly demonstrated God's protection over their lives.

After all their perils in southern Ethiopia, they eventually arrived at the Kenyan border and were accepted as refugees. God continued showing them great favor through a church in Ft. Wayne, Indiana, which sponsored them as refugees in America. Thanks to Deme's engineering skills and their motivation, they started a factory and supported themselves and several employees.

In 1991, the Derg fell, as did many other communist governments around the world at that time in history. The door opened for Marta and Deme to return to Ethiopia, and they pledged to use their resources to help their native country for the rest of their lives. And thus began Project Mercy, an integrated rural development program. Located in the remote village of Yetebon among the Gurage (goo' rah gay) tribe southwest of Addis Ababa, Project

Mercy's outreaches consist of a large school, a modern hospital, a church, vocational training, a large home for orphans, farming, etc. This impressive project regularly attracts international attention.

With its American headquarters based in Ft. Wayne, Indiana, Project Mercy is located just across the state line from where Peggy grew up near Van Wert, Ohio. It is also very near the largest local church of our denomination, located in Bluffton, Indiana. Marta is well-known in that area, as she speaks and engages people with a lot of charisma. Several of Peggy's extended family members and many members of the Apostolic Christian Church had heard Marta speak on Christian radio and at women's breakfasts, read her articles in the press, and read her book.

When these friends and relatives heard of our plans to move to Ethiopia as missionaries, they encouraged us to contact Marta and visit Yetebon to report back on how things were going with Project Mercy. They sent us Marta's book, her Ethiopian telephone number, and other information about Project Mercy. Some of our friends appeared to be more interested in our becoming acquainted with Project Mercy than in our relationship with Wycliffe Bible Translators.

Peggy tried to call Marta a couple of times after we initially arrived in Ethiopia but was unable to reach her. We didn't place making this contact with an unknown person as a very high priority, considering our busy schedules and commitment to SIL. However, when we returned to the U.S. for our first vacation and reported we had not made contact with Marta, disappointment clearly showed on some of our friends' faces. They renewed their efforts, supplying us with more information and more telephone numbers to contact Project Mercy in Ethiopia.

We returned to Ethiopia after that vacation with renewed determination to find this "elusive" Marta. After trying and trying, finally in early January 2003 Peggy made telephone contact with her. Peggy explained to Marta how people back in the U.S. had encouraged us to meet her and that since our return to Ethiopia we had been diligently trying to contact her. Marta was pleasant enough to Peggy but stated that she and Deme were very busy and simply did not have time to meet with us. Although somewhat disappointed by this response, at least we could report back to our friends in the States that we had tried and eventually made contact.

Along the way, we asked several of our acquaintances in Ethiopia if they had ever heard of Yetebon or Project Mercy. No one had. Not realizing Yetebon's extreme remoteness (actually it isn't even a village, but rather an area name) we wondered if such a place as Yetebon really existed.

But God had plans for Marta and Deme and us. We were at a "town meeting" at the U.S. Embassy in late February, called by the U.S. ambassador to exchange information with American citizens. While we waited for Ambassador Aurelia Brazeal to appear, a somewhat elderly couple came and sat down in the chairs next to me. I extended my hand to the lady and introduced myself as "Gary." She smiled and said her name was "Marta" and introduced the man next to her as her husband "Deme." As the cliché goes, one could have knocked me over with a feather. When I explained who we were and that Peggy had talked to her on the phone, she profusely apologized for not being able to meet with us at that time.

Long after the town meeting ended that evening, the four of us still stood inside the U.S. Embassy compound talking, comparing acquaintances, and discussing our respective work in Ethiopia. We could hardly believe we had finally caught up with Marta and Deme.

We became instant friends. They insisted we accompany them out to Yetebon the following weekend. Of course, we agreed. On that Saturday morning they picked us up very early, around 5:00, to drive the five hours out to Yetebon. (Later, when the roads were improved and asphalted, we traveled to Yetebon from Addis Ababa in two and a half hours.) Marta had prepared breakfast, and we ate it in the car on the way.

Arriving at Yetebon we were genuinely impressed by its beautiful setting. It was situated at an altitude similar to Addis Ababa (about 8,000 feet, or 2,500 meters), and the majestic Gurage Mountains stood another 2,000 feet (650 meters) above that. Deme and Marta gave us a detailed tour of all activities—the school with its 1,000 students, orphanage, vocational training, gardens, farms, and the unfinished hospital.

Local kitchen workers prepared delicious meals that always included a variety of Ethiopian food and "European" food. We enjoyed the comfortable guest house and marveled that a place like this existed in such a remote area of Africa. At the end of our stay we returned to Addis Ababa with not a doubt in our minds that Yetebon was a real and vibrant place.

Later that spring Peggy and I found ourselves with a four-day weekend and nowhere to go. We called Marta and asked if we could go out to Yetebon and soak up the beauty and ambience of that place during our holiday. She agreed, so Peggy and I drove out and found it just as we remembered. We met some of the amiable young volunteers from the U.S., got acquainted with the workers and some of the orphans, took hikes up in the mountains, and enjoyed a relaxing and special time.

Marta and Deme came from Addis Ababa to Yetebon over that long weekend, and one evening after supper we got into a deep God-ordained conversation with them. After about two hours of discussion, during which I never even thought about the passing of time, Marta abruptly stopped and asked, "Can you believe this? We've been sitting here talking for two hours, and we have not been interrupted even once." Only later did we realize how unusual that really was.

During that conversation we discussed with Deme and Marta our desire to move to rural Ethiopia and get more directly involved with Ethiopians. Considering our downward-spiraling relationship with the SIL director and his wife, and also having been exposed to the poverty and desperate plight of the people of rural Ethiopia, getting to the countryside increasingly became a desire of ours.

And, as mentioned previously, my job at SIL was starting to resemble an 8 to 5 office job, which really wasn't what I had anticipated as a missionary. We saw ourselves somewhere other than in the big city, living a missionary life more like what Uncle Melvin Huber or my cousin Luke lived in Brazil. Sitting in an office in a city of four million residents (Addis Ababa) didn't fit our picture of "missionary life." Peggy and I felt there should be more sacrifice on our part than what we were giving.

Many people might think leaving family, friends, a comfortable job, and the American lifestyle to go to the third poorest country in the world would be a big enough sacrifice. The strange thing about human nature, though, is that once we become acclimated to a certain lifestyle, regardless of how rich or poor, we strive for an even more fulfilling lifestyle. For us that meant giving up some of the "luxuries" of living in Addis Ababa and going to serve the needy people in the rural areas.

Our conversation with Deme and Marta that evening covered a lot of territory, and we felt really special to have had their undivided attention for such a long time. After a wonderful four days at Yetebon we returned to Addis Ababa and our SIL work.

Then, much to our surprise, the tables turned and Marta called us. She asked if we had time to get together and visit. Peggy and I quickly agreed to meet with her and Deme.

Even though they are Americans by passport, they are still Ethiopians by DNA. Instead of broaching the subject directly, they sort of circled it in the Ethiopian style and after two hours eventually got to the point.

"Were you really serious about what you said at Yetebon about getting more involved with development out in the countryside?" Marta asked.

"Of course, we are serious about that."

She then floored us with the question, "Gary, would you be willing to be the administrator of the hospital you saw out there, and Peggy, would you be the facilities manager?"

Whoa, Lord! I thought, What's going on here? Our situation at SIL is going downhill; we have a desire to get more directly involved with Ethiopians; and now we are presented with this opportunity; is this Your will? Is this what You have in mind for us? Isn't this a pretty big step all at once?

Letting them know we really appreciated their confidence in us, Peggy and I asked for time to think, pray, and discuss this opportunity. They understood and agreed.

My prayer shot to heaven: "Lord, I'm just an Illinois farm boy. What in the world would make me think I could start up and run a hospital out in the middle of nowhere Ethiopia? Surely there is someone better qualified than me."

Of all the hundreds of thoughts racing through our minds (How would our Wycliffe supporters react to this? Could we live in the countryside with no electricity, telephone, or e-mail? Would we be able to handle being the only white people out in that remote place?), Sam's education concerned us the most.

Little did we know that God had that little issue already taken care of.

As I struggled with all these considerations, I remembered that Moses had misgivings and a lack of confidence similar to mine, as expressed in Exodus 4:11-13 (NIV): "The LORD said to him [Moses], 'Who gave man his mouth? Who makes him deaf or mute? Who gives him sight or makes him blind? Is it not I, the LORD? Now go; I will help you speak and will teach you what to say.' But Moses said, 'O Lord, please send someone else to do it.'"

As God has led me on my missionary journey, I have experienced similar kinds of misgivings many times. Each new task looks so big and overwhelming. It always seems life would be so much

easier simply by staying in my current position, safely in my comfort zone. However, each time God has made it uncomfortable for
me and perfectly clear He has a new job for Peggy and me to do. I
have gained great courage from the dialogue between Moses and
God many times over. Even though I ask God to "send someone
else to do it," He reminds me that He is the One who made me
and gifted me with specific capabilities. He will always see me
through. And, even though I have been faint of heart on numerous
occasions, He has never stranded me.

CHAPTER 21

Sam's Education Dream Comes True

We never actually anticipated Sam enrolling in Rift Valley Academy, even after his expressed desire to stay in Kijabe, Kenya, when we visited Mark and Pam Hodel as we passed through Kenya on our way back to Ethiopia. But what are our plans compared to God's plans, and what are our thoughts compared to God's thoughts?

Returning from Safari, we arrived in Ethiopia just in time for Sam to begin the third quarter of his grade 7 school year at Bingham Academy. Prior to our arrival the seventh grade class was already full. The only reason the Bingham Academy administration allowed Sam to enroll was because SIL was a sustaining mission for Bingham. All children of parents who were members of a sustaining mission received guaranteed enrollment. If we had not been SIL members, Sam could not have enrolled, and no other good alternative existed in Addis Ababa. Also fortunately for us, Bingham operated on the American system, which was designed to prepare him well for higher education in the U.S.

During Sam's eighth grade a new school director arrived on the scene—David Hicks from Australia. Toward the end of the school year Mr. Hicks called a meeting of the high school parents. He announced that the following year Bingham Academy was going to switch to the British IGCSE (International General Certificate of Secondary Education) system.

To Peggy and me that was just another acronym. We had no idea how those letters would impact Sam's education. After having completed our own educations up through the college level, having had two daughters graduate from high school, and Sam having completed primary school, we knew educators regularly threw around acronyms for new educational methods. We didn't give this announcement much thought.

Red flags started to wave, though, when other parents started pulling their kids out of Bingham and enrolling them in other schools. But Peggy and I, in our naïveté, blissfully went along with the program. When ninth grade began to unfold under the new British system, we found ourselves totally unprepared for its effect on Sam. Our son, who had always gotten As and Bs, was now getting Cs and praying to avoid the Ds. He studied late into the night but never felt confident he was studying the right things. The classroom methods, homework, tests—everything about school—left him frustrated. All aspects of school felt unfamiliar to him. And Sam's stress became our stress.

More and more high school students withdrew from Bingham. We didn't know any really good alternatives for Sam anywhere in Ethiopia. In desperation we contacted Rift Valley Academy. Even though we were aware that many African missionary parents practically put their kids on the RVA waiting list upon conception, we decided to try to enroll Sam for the next school year. The admissions officer, Mrs. Prinie Stark, told us the upcoming tenth grade class at RVA had been filled for months; however, we could still put Sam's name on the waiting list just in case a spot opened up.

In December, SIL sent me to Nairobi for a financial audit of the Ethiopia branch. During the week of my visit there was a Kenyan holiday, meaning no audit work that day. I used that opportunity to go to Kijabe to visit our friends Mark and Pam once again. While there I hand-delivered Sam's application and accompanying fee to Prinie. I explained Sam's school situation and shared with her our prayers for a miracle for his admittance to RVA. She held out absolutely no hope that Sam could be admitted.

From submitting the application in December 2002 until the first week of June 2003, there was no progress with Sam's application. Finally, as the school year drew to a close, we essentially gave up hope. At that point we had formally decided to move to Yetebon to work at the Project Mercy Hospital, even though the rural environment offered no educational opportunities for Sam. The educational standards of the Ethiopian schools did not measure up either to our expectations or the standards of American universities. Therefore, we started looking for a boarding school for Sam in Addis Ababa.

After one last e-mail to Prinie inquiring about Sam's status, she wrote back saying that a boy in ninth grade had dropped out of the school. RVA tries to balance its student body based on male-female ratios, diversity, etc. So the replacing student needed to be a male. Six male applicants met the qualifications, and Sam was one of them. A glimmer of hope!

Shortly thereafter, Prinie wrote and told us they had selected Sam to enter tenth grade at RVA the next school year. We learned this good news just two weeks before we left for the U.S. for our annual visit. We praised God for this miracle. Again, I prayed, "Lord, I'm just an Illinois farm boy. It's amazing to me how You grant my family favor by working these things out for us. You really must care for even the sparrows."

Sam, a typical teenage boy, rarely showed emotion, especially regarding educational issues. Upon hearing of his admission to RVA, though, he could hardly contain his excitement. But this news also meant we needed to do a lot of things in a big hurry to prepare Sam for living and studying in Kenya during the next school year.

Two things of real significance stand out regarding this turn of events. The first was we had determined, during the time we were searching out which foreign country to serve in, that we wanted Sam to be able to live at home with us. We did not want him to have to go off to another country to boarding school. But, upon receiving news of his admission to RVA, all three of us rejoiced that he would be in another country attending a boarding school.

And, secondly, after Safari Sam had made the unusual comment that he wanted to stay at RVA and attend school while Peggy and I returned to Ethiopia. He saw something about that school he really liked. His wish to study there came true.

CHAPTER 22

Our Life-Changing Decision

After much prayer and discussion, weighing the pros and cons, Peggy and I agreed the clear signs God had laid on our hearts regarding a career change could not be ignored.

One sign was that our jobs at SIL had turned into somewhat routine 8 to 5 jobs resembling our secular jobs back in the States.

A second was we had always envisioned ourselves serving the Lord as missionaries in a setting other than a large metropolitan city. We saw ourselves living a more basic lifestyle in a traditional missionary setting.

Third, for some inexplicable reason we found ourselves in an untenable situation with the leadership of SIL. No matter how frequently we apologized and submitted to micromanagement of our jobs, we could never do things well enough for the director and his wife.

Fourth, our serendipitous meeting with Marta and Deme also led us to believe that God had new plans for us. Our friends back in the States had insisted we meet Marta and Deme. But our attempts to contact them had failed until God divinely intervened and caused us to meet at the U.S. Embassy. Shortly after our first meetings with them, they offered us the most challenging jobs imaginable in the Ethiopian countryside, working with Christians in a Muslim tribal group.

Reasoning that God through these signs was encouraging us to proceed with the invitation to move to Yetebon, we requested another meeting with Marta and Deme. We wanted to ask more questions about the proposed work at the hospital. They reminded us of the hardships of living full-time in such a remote area without telephone, electricity, or e-mail. Butajira, the nearest town, was six miles (ten kilometers) away; however, driving there from Yetebon required nearly half an hour because of the terrible road. Butajira offered only the most basic of services. But, they told us, at least we could find a telephone there, along with a couple of very slow and virus-ridden Internet cafés. We told them we understood these challenges, but we had confidence that God would take care of us. He had not brought us to this point by accident or coincidence.

So we accepted their offer.

Because I didn't want our resignation from Wycliffe Bible Translators to be tainted by the SIL director's opinions and biases, we did not tell him about our decision to leave the Ethiopia branch. Our chain-of-command ran up through Wycliffe USA, headquartered in Orlando, Florida. I felt it was appropriate that they be the first to know, so I sent our resignation letter directly to Orlando.

Knowing we had the Project Mercy opportunity in our back pocket made our remaining time at SIL much more tolerable. The director and his wife didn't know of our resignation prior to our leaving for the U.S. for our vacation that summer. However, they continued to use all means available to them to make sure we knew our places and that we understood we could make only the simplest decisions without checking with them first. Anytime anyone came to us for advice or help was perceived by them as a threat to their authority.

We felt that if the other SIL members started to avoid us or show disrespect, then perhaps all or part of the fault was ours. But that never happened. Our good relationships with all other branch members continued to thrive and remain strong. No one else at the branch did even one thing to show they did not respect or trust us. To this day all of those friendships are as strong as or stronger than ever.

My stomach was churning with anxiety the morning of Peggy's and my performance evaluations, referred to in the introduction to this book. The Spirit told me to be prepared for something bad. The director and his wife wanted to administer our AMPRs (Annual Member Planning and Review) together with both Peggy and me present at the same time.

They told us they would not allow Peggy to re-assume her member services manager position and that I was on one-year probation. Only by being extremely careful and submissive and reading books on culture shock could I earn my job back. Looking back after a number of years, that meeting made no logical sense. Unfortunately, though, it was our careers and reputations that were at stake at the time.

Even knowing we weren't going to continue with SIL, being told the things we were told in such a degrading manner shook us to our foundations. And, because there was no substantiation for what they said, the hurt cut even deeper. Believing with all our hearts that they fabricated our negative evaluations to avoid an imagined threat to their positions, Peggy and I left the meeting choked up with our eyes red and wet from tears.

Never before in our lives did we experience so many major family changes in such a short time as we did during our summer vacation of 2003. I am still amazed by how God went ahead of us and perfectly put everything in place.

Since Sam would be living in Kenya when we returned to Africa, the reality of having an empty nest earlier than planned hit us hard. Losing him from our household in Ethiopia was going to be sad, but we knew he wanted to change schools and that it was God's clear will.

Our daughter Angie, engaged to be married, planned to move out of our condo to a house she and her fiancé, Walter Reedy, had purchased. That meant our condo would be empty and we needed a caretaker for it.

Also during our visit to the States, we needed to visit the Project Mercy Headquarters in Ft. Wayne, Indiana, to arrange the logistics for our transfer from Wycliffe. Sam Myhre, Marta's oldest son from her marriage to the Norwegian missionary, managed the U.S. office of Project Mercy. Sam and his staff helped us significantly with the transition. As the first "supported" missionaries working alongside Project Mercy, we spent a lot of time that summer helping to design the system of receiving funds in our names and maintaining our account records.

We needed to know the names and addresses of anyone who sent in funds toward our work, so we could thank them and track our account balance. This information was essential not only for our personal record-keeping, but the IRS was also interested for income and social security tax reasons. Wire transfer capabilities either to our bank in the U.S. or our account in Ethiopia had to be arranged. Project Mercy blessed us by not deducting any administrative fees from our income, while Wycliffe had taken 10 percent for administration. That meant more money coming through the system for our mission work.

Over time we were able to work out all the logistics of transferring to Project Mercy and preparing to work at Yetebon when we returned to Ethiopia. However, the event we thought would be the most difficult of that fateful summer turned out to be the greatest blessing. I felt, without a doubt, that we should personally visit the Florida headquarters of Wycliffe Bible Translators. As our sending organization, we were ultimately accountable to them, and we needed to personally explain the events leading up to our resignation and lay out our plans for the future. This personal touch was especially important to us as we had, in some way or other, been affiliated with Wycliffe since the late 1970s. We felt a great affinity with them.

After setting up a meeting with Wycliffe's personnel administrator, Nancy Lange, we flew to Orlando. Nancy and her husband, Roger, had been overseas missionaries themselves for many years. We remembered meeting Roger at Wycliffe's Quest in California in 1989, when he worked as one of the administrators of that program.

We entered Nancy's office a little nervous about the reason for our visit and also without knowing what negative information from Ethiopia preceded us. But her warmth and grasp of our situation immediately put us at ease. As we had suspected, she had read everything the Ethiopia SIL director had written about us. We thought she might have negative preconceived notions concerning us, but on that count we were badly mistaken.

Shortly after we started telling our story, Nancy called in the vice-president of personnel. They both listened intently to what we had to say. When we finished, we figured they might admonish us and question our behavior within the Ethiopia branch and perhaps even threaten us with some punishment. Instead they did something entirely unexpected. They left the room for a moment and conferred with each other. When they returned, they looked at us and said they were tired of all the American missionaries who were leaving the "Euro-centric" Ethiopian branch because of problems with the director.

We were floored!

We learned that almost all of our American friends who had left the Ethiopia branch during our stay in Addis Ababa had come back and also complained about the director. Right there on the spot they decided that no more American missionaries would be sent to the Ethiopian branch until the current director left his post. And that turned out to be exactly what happened. Only one American family, already in the pipeline, went to Addis Ababa until after the director departed the branch and Ethiopia. Several of our SIL friends wondered why they were having such a difficult time recruiting Americans. We couldn't say anything, but we knew the reason!

Nancy Lange didn't stop there in blessing us. After showing a lot of understanding and empathy for our situation, she asked about our next steps. Would we be willing to transfer to another country or perhaps return to the U.S. and work in one of the Wycliffe offices there? Wycliffe was very eager to retain us in some capacity.

We explained how God had divinely intervened and led us to Project Mercy to start up a hospital in the countryside of Ethiopia. She understood. Then she offered to do something that likely had not been done before. If it had been done before, it was very rare. She offered to write a letter to all our financial supporters describing our plans to leave Wycliffe Bible Translators with the full blessing of the organization. And, in the letter she wanted to encourage our supporters to continue supporting us at Project Mercy. We accepted her gracious offer, and she followed through.

This letter was a very meaningful expression from Wycliffe, and it blessed us tremendously at a time when we felt we were at the bottom of the pit. I am reproducing it here verbatim:

Dear [Name],

After much thought and prayerful consideration, Gary and Peggy Ifft will be taking a Leave of Absence from Wycliffe Bible Translators. They will no longer be in active service with us effective October 1, 2003. We are thankful for the years that Gary and Peggy worked with us.

They made a valuable contribution towards completing the Bible translation needs of the people who do not yet have the Word in their own language. Gary and Peggy have served in administrative roles in Ethiopia, supporting the language teams working among the 86 languages of that country.

Thank you for your partnership with the Iffts. I know they appreciate your support and prayers. I want to express our sincere appreciation also. They will continue to work in Ethiopia with another mission, Project Mercy, as the directors of a new hospital. It has just been built, and will be opening soon. We encourage you to continue to support them financially also, by sending your contributions to:

Project Mercy
7011 Ardmore Ave
Ft. Wayne, IN 46809

Funds designated for them which are received by Wycliffe during October, November, and December will continue to be forwarded to them; however, we encourage you to move your support to their new organization as soon as possible.

Your encouragement for the work of Wycliffe through Gary and Peggy has been deeply appreciated. Please continue to pray for Gary and Peggy as they undergo their transition period.

Blessings,
Nancy Lange
Personnel Administrator

What a wonderful demonstration of support that was! During 2002 and 2003 the dotcom bubble had burst. Financial giving to charitable organizations fell off precipitously, and Wycliffe was no exception. As a matter of fact, several SIL projects in Ethiopia had to be canceled or reduced due to lack of funding. One mission organization's suggestion that financial supporters send money to another mission organization truly demonstrated unselfishness and sacrifice.

God blessed us with a strong and loyal support base. I don't think we lost a single financial supporter in the transition. Some people later told us they initially had supported us because of their interest in Bible translation; however, they also believed in us as individuals and would continue to support us at Project Mercy.

Nancy also took care of all correspondence with the director and the personnel manager of the Ethiopia branch, a voice of authority regarding how our situation should be handled. They could try to manipulate us, but they would not manipulate the largest Wycliffe office in the world.

In spite of our experience within the office in Addis Ababa, we love and remain as loyal to Wycliffe as ever. It is truly a great organization performing one of the most needed services in God's Kingdom.

CHAPTER 23

Post-Wycliffe

Angie's wedding ranked as the most special family event of that 2003 summer vacation. The church was beautifully decorated; hundreds of relatives and friends came from all over; the bride was radiant; and the groom was handsome. My first experience of giving away the bride left me torn with emotions over its significance. I was proud to do that as a father; however, it did leave an ache in my heart for our firstborn to be leaving our home.

Our looming departure for Ethiopia on Monday, September 8, made the event especially poignant, since the wedding took place on Saturday, only two days before. Walter and Angie did not leave immediately on their honeymoon but stayed around to be with us and open their gifts on the Sunday in between.

Just before we left the U.S. God amazingly took care of another of our concerns. After Angie moved out of our condo we didn't want it standing unoccupied for a year until we returned to Bloomington the following summer. Not wanting to place the caretaker responsibilities on Walter's and Angie's shoulders, but also not wanting to rent to strangers whose home care and maintenance skills were unknown to us, left us in a dilemma we wrestled with during the final days of our vacation.

As Peggy and I went out early one morning for what was probably our final walk of that summer, we made it only a short distance down our street when a van stopped and the driver called to us. Since I normally go out for exercise without my glasses, I couldn't see clearly who it was. We walked over to the van and found a former neighbor from our Towanda subdivision who was also a former fellow State Farm employee, Bill Roe.

"Bill, we thought you and your wife moved down south after you retired. What in the world are you doing back in Bloomington?"

"Well, what are you two doing here? I thought you guys were somewhere in Africa."

"We're back here at our condo for a few weeks this summer. Angie is getting married Saturday, and we also had a lot of other business to take care of. What brings you to our neighborhood?"

"You see, State Farm asked me to come back out of retirement for a little while and help out with a project in my old department. I'm currently staying at the extended-stay hotel on the south edge of town, but I would like something that feels a little more like home. I'm looking into renting that condo over there."

"Why don't you rent our condo? We leave to go back to Ethiopia on Monday. It's fully furnished. We'll let you rent it for a lot less than those guys probably will," we replied, knowing he would be a responsible tenant. He and his wife had owned a beautiful home in our former subdivision.

We showed him our house, and he eagerly accepted our offer. It was a match made in heaven, and the problem of caring for our condo for the next year was taken care of.

"Thank you (again), Lord!"

With all the items on our to-do list for the summer now checked off, we turned our thoughts toward returning to Africa and our new work.

We flew the long way around to get back to Ethiopia. In Amsterdam we switched from KLM to Kenya Airways. Because Nairobi is their hub, Kenya Airways allowed us to break our flight itinerary in Nairobi for no extra charge. This allowed us a couple of days to go out Rift Valley Academy in Kijabe to settle Sam in his new school.

Due to Angie's wedding on September 6, Sam was very late for the start of school. Since it was a miracle he got into RVA on such late notice, it was with trepidation that we wrote to Prinie Stark to tell her Sam would arrive two weeks after the semester began. We held our breath, anticipating her answer. To our relief Prinie wrote back affirming that his late arrival was acceptable if Sam made up all the work he missed. He willingly agreed since he so badly wanted to attend RVA.

Sam was very pleased about his new arrangements, except for that part about making up two weeks' worth of work. Having grown up with two considerably older sisters (Angie, eleven years older, and Becky, eight), he often complained that we as parents had deprived him of the brother he so badly wanted. He saw other boys in the neighborhood with brothers to play with, but he had none.

In his dorm, filled with twenty-four testosterone-charged teenage boys, he found the "brothers" he had desired for so long. Afterwards when he came to visit us in Ethiopia his eyes regularly lit up as he told us of his experiences with sports, pranks, and the camaraderie of his fellow students.

CHAPTER 24

Yetebon Life

With Sam safely settled in at the boarding school in Kenya, we traveled on to Ethiopia to begin the next chapter of our lives. Once in Addis Ababa we immediately made preparations to move to our new home in the countryside. We knew it was God's will and absolutely the right thing to do, but, boy, we are still human. Can one have confidence and trepidation at the same time? We sure did.

Any move is a big job, but this one presented extra challenges because again we found ourselves facing a major downsize to a tiny house. Project Mercy sent two flatbed Isuzu trucks to carry our belongings out to Yetebon.

Before our house in the hospital staff housing complex was completed, Marta assigned us a room in the Project Mercy guest house. In the guest house we had only two twin beds and a rod to hang our clothes on, along with a bathroom that contained a shower. We took our meals in the dining room with the other supervisory personnel and any guests who were visiting Yetebon. This common dining arrangement usually led to interesting conversations and was a good introduction to Project Mercy and the Yetebon area.

However, we were very eager to move to our little house near the hospital. We looked forward to the privacy of setting up our own home. Our furniture and personal belongings awaited us in a warehouse. We worried about rats getting into our things, as well as dust and bird droppings.

We rejoiced when the day arrived that our house (one-half of a duplex in a row of two-bedroom duplex houses) was ready for us to move in. It, of course, was brand new, with us being the first residents. The paint was fresh, and the landscaping had not yet been tackled. We had no electricity or phone—no utilities except for running water.

And getting running water to our house in Yetebon was a minor miracle in itself. Deme is a good engineer who understands the importance of a sustainable water supply. When he and Marta set up the facilities in Yetebon at the inception of Project Mercy, they searched for a reliable source of water. A river flows past the Project Mercy site; however, in the dry season it dries up, or nearly so. In the rainy season it can be a roaring cascade of water sweeping huge rocks down the mountain.

Deme and Marta had tried drilling wells but found no success in the horrifically rocky soil of that area. As an alternative they considered bringing water down from the mountains, if they could find a reliable spring. They consulted a group of village elders to see if they knew of a spring up in the mountains that never went dry. The elders put their heads together and said, yes, there was a spring above Project Mercy, which even their great-grandfathers had said never dried up. But if Project Mercy commandeered that spring, they would have no source of water to use for their own houses and farms.

Eventually, Project Mercy and the village elders worked out a compromise, a win-win solution. Project Mercy would cap off the spring with a concrete bunker-like collection facility, but volunteered to provide spigots at various locations down the mountain for the villagers to use. Instead of dipping their water out of a muddy pit, they merely had to turn on a spigot to get healthy, clean water.

This water collection bunker was situated over two miles (approximately three kilometers) from the Project Mercy main compound. In what is truly an engineering marvel, teams of workers dug a trench from the bunker all the way down to the Project Mercy compound. The very rocky soil made digging difficult and even treacherous. At one point they ran across a rock so big that they couldn't find the ends of it. Dynamite cleared that problem out of the way. Four-inch PVC pipe was laid in the trench, and all of the Project Mercy facilities had clean mountain spring water available to them.

In our early days at Yetebon, when we weren't as busy as we became later, I had a great idea for improving my language capability. I estimated my Amharic proficiency to be about the second or third grade level. Feeling a little foolish and intimidated, I asked the headmaster of the school if it would be possible for me to sit in on the third grade Amharic class each day. After recovering from his shock and suppressing his laughter, he agreed it would be fine and gave me the schedule for the third grade class.

I loved that class. The students, ranging in age from eight to eighteen, probably never did understand why a gray-haired fifty-something man was in the classroom with them. They cooperated, though, and went along with the program. As I love learning languages, I looked forward to that class each day. I even looked forward to the walk from our house near the hospital down and up the mountain to school.

Teacher Getahun felt special, I think, for having me in his classroom. However, he did not defer to me or treat me special. I had my assigned desk near the front of the classroom of seventy-five students. One girl, who sat in the desk next to me, was very bright and became my special friend, always greeting me when I entered the school compound.

Usually on test days I skipped class. One week, though, Getahun implored me to come and take the test with the rest of the students. I should have seen it coming. The next day in class, before he handed our test papers back, I saw him preparing to make a little speech. He held up my test paper, which had a grade of 70 (out of 100), and told the students that this was one of the best papers of the class. He asked them how a foreigner who had been in the country only a few years could receive a better grade than most of them. He used that comparison to admonish them to try harder, as they were Ethiopians and should be performing at a higher level in his class. Admittedly, for most of the students of that area, Amharic was their second language, with their first being their tribal language, Gurage.

I was so embarrassed I could have crawled under my chair and stayed there for the remainder of the class period. I thoroughly relished attending that class, though, until my hospital duties became so great that I could no longer devote the time each day. But for years afterwards, I considered that a special time and longed to return to those simpler days.

CHAPTER 25

Our Hospital Work Begins

In 2003, when we moved to Yetebon, there was a terrible famine in that area. Project Mercy devoted all of its resources to keeping people alive. Its trucks made their daily round-trips to feeding centers for miles around, taking Atmit (a kind of dried-powder porridge that, once mixed with water and drunk three times a day, provides all the nutrients necessary for a good diet), cooking oil, grains, etc., to the starving people.

Project Mercy also set up a temporary clinic for malnourished babies in its compound. Dr. Mebratu, an Ethiopian general practitioner, and Dr. Penny, an American doctor, had 108 starving babies on their hands when we arrived. Soon the population of babies outgrew the capacity of the clinic building. Project Mercy staff set up tents to hold more babies, along with a mother or father for each. The doctors and nurses weighed each baby every day and gave them Atmit eight times a day. This action on the part of Project Mercy saved many little precious lives.

The situation tore at Peggy's and my hearts. In addition to daily observing the malnourished babies, we also visited some of the feeding centers. It pained us to see long lines of people waiting for rice, wheat, or oil. Even the most calloused heart could not help but have compassion for all the poor people and would try to do everything possible to help them.

But that is exactly what Marta asked us not to do. She asked us not to get involved with the feeding programs or caring for the babies, but rather focus on opening the hospital. She lamented how "that hospital has been sitting up there unfinished for way too long." The hospital was situated one mile (or one and a half kilometers) up the mountain from the lower, main compound, where the school was located. It still needed quite a bit of construction work (masonry, electrical, plumbing) in order for the building itself to be finished. Many huge shipping crates sat around in the corridors and in some of the rooms. We could only imagine the medical treasures waiting for us to place them in their proper places within the hospital.

Regarding staff, Dr. Penny returned to the U.S. shortly after we arrived. The only doctor we had was Dr. Mebratu, and he was focused on keeping starving babies alive. He did not have time to help us with the hospital. In addition, we had twenty-seven PHCAs (Primary Health Care Assistants). The PHCAs were young people from the community who had received training on the basics of medical care from an American lady, Barbara Hood, who had previously been a hospital administrator in the States. Several months before, two rural Catholic hospitals gave them the opportunity to do hands-on hospital work. They received training on everything from assisting the nurses (emptying bedpans, checking IVs, taking temperatures) to janitorial duties (cleaning, incinerating), to stocking drugs, to registering patients and collecting money.

Unfortunately for us in those early days, all the PHCAs were involved in working at the feeding centers. So the real hospital staff was, for better or for worse, Peggy and me.

Marta told me that my office was to be in the lower compound in a room shared with the school secretary, Dr. Mebratu, and a young American volunteer writing grant proposals. For a chronically organized person like me, that setup was a disaster. Each day

I contended for a chair, part of a table, and a few precious minutes of computer time. Most of the time I used my own laptop, but I occasionally needed to get on the Project Mercy computer to access some hospital documents.

One positive result came out of sharing the cramped office quarters. One day when I entered my shared office and wanted to use the Project Mercy computer, an attractive young lady was already using it. I introduced myself and asked her name and what she was doing.

She responded in Amharic, "My name is Mahelet, and I am the school secretary. I need to use the computer to type examinations for the teachers."

It seemed that her test-typing was higher priority than my work, so I didn't press the issue of my using the computer further at that time. As I got to know her better over the next couple of weeks, I realized she was a dedicated Christian woman, the wife of one of the teachers. She seemed to be very knowledgeable with the computer and seemed to have good secretarial skills.

A couple of months later when I needed a secretary at the hospital I asked Marta if I could hire one. "Or," I said, "I could just take Mahelet," with my fingers crossed.

Marta replied, "Mahelet's English isn't so good. I will find you a better secretary."

After nothing happened for some weeks I again reminded Marta of my need for a secretary. She confessed that she needed to find me one and said she would send a secretary to the hospital shortly. One day Mahelet came to my hospital office and said she was sent up by Marta to be my secretary. Prayer answered!

I was happy, and Mahelet proved to be a very capable secretary, although most of our conversations required me to practice my Amharic language skills. We worked well together, and I appreciated her cooperative attitude. Her weakness was playing virus-laden music CDs, which were freely shared among the Ethiopians.

One day when her computer ground to a halt, I ran an antivirus program and found over 2,700 virus infections.

When I finally got really fed up with sharing an office with so many people and coming in each day to find my stack of papers rearranged and out of order, I told Peggy I was moving my office to the hospital. I had seen an old metal desk in a storeroom stacked sky-high with lots of old beds and furniture and other junk. I dug out the desk and claimed it as my own. (It was a metal American "principal's desk" from ages past that weighed about 300 pounds.) I also found a steno chair and a file cabinet for letter-sized papers. In Ethiopia we use A4 paper, which is longer and narrower than American letter size, and it doesn't fit in an 8 1/2 x 11 inch file. But I needed the business-like appearance in my office that a file cabinet provided.

I placed those three pieces of furniture in the corner administrative office, along with a couple of miscellaneous chairs I found, and proudly announced, "We are open for business." Not medical business, but rather hospital start-up business. With no electricity I could work on my laptop only as long as the battery held out.

Claiming my office turned out to be one of the best decisions I ever made regarding the hospital. It demonstrated to the Project Mercy staff that we were serious about having a hospital. Even some visitors who wandered all the way off the main road six miles away stopped in to see this marvelous hospital, soon to open.

And marvelous it was. Marta and Deme have an eye for quality. They imported first-class equipment, machines, and instruments from Europe and Japan.

As activities picked up at the hospital site, the residents of Yetebon and surrounding communities eagerly anticipated the hospital's opening. Our catchment area consisted of 75,000 people who had never had health care available to them before. In order to see a medical practitioner, other than the local witch doctors or traditional healers, they had to travel over treacherous roads to faraway places that they could hardly afford. Most of those villagers earned less than $80 U.S. per year! The vegetables and grains they raised on their little farms provided the subsistence for their families.

Slowly, slowly, the famine subsided. And gradually the PHCAs were allowed to come back to the work for which they had been trained, that of working in the hospital. It was Peggy's job, as facilities manager, to keep them occupied. But keeping so many people productively engaged when the hospital had not yet opened and there were no patients to care for proved challenging. She had them scrub, mop, dust, sweep, and then do it all over again. And, after she eventually got all twenty-seven PHCAs under her authority, some days she simply had them pick up rocks from the hospital compound.

When we received enough PHCAs at the hospital to really get serious about becoming a medical facility, I made my second major pronouncement. I said, "This is a hospital, not a museum. Today we begin opening these crates to see what we have here."

The staff was stunned. For two years they had walked, mopped, and swept around those crates.

Was I really going to open them?

Was I authorized?

My, that was a big job. With my hammer and crowbar I began opening crates. It took several days to get everything unpacked.

Oxygen concentrators were in one crate; in another, the anesthesia machine; in others, the surgical instruments; in still more, the operating room lights; and on and on. Christmas arrived early in Yetebon that year.

Peggy and I found about fifty used hospital beds, donated from and American hospital, along with rails, in several heaps in one of the storerooms. We, along with the PHCAs, set them up in the wards. That's when I discovered a big difference between an Illinois farm boy and an Ethiopian boy. I grew up, under the tutelage of my dad, knowing how to use wrenches, screwdrivers, tape measures, and pliers as second nature. These Ethiopian kids had never held such magical tools in their hands before. I chuckled under my breath watching them try to use something as simple as a wrench. One of my greatest legacies may be that today, in Yetebon, Ethiopia, there are a bunch of young adults who are comfortable using a ratchet wrench.

With the help of some American volunteers I made great progress on the policies, procedures, and forms for the hospital. Even though I had been in hospitals as a visitor, a patient, and even as a lab technician in the U.S. Army, I had no idea at all of how many forms are required to run a hospital. Peggy and I visited many hospitals around Ethiopia, collecting as many of their forms as we could talk them out of. I knew we would need X-ray forms, laboratory forms, and even some of the forms the nurses use like history sheets, vital signs, input-output log, and progress notes. However, it didn't dawn on me that we needed death certificates, birth certificates, consent forms, operating room schedules, and, of course, cash receipts and ledger books.

I became overwhelmed with forms, thinking I could never conquer the task of designing them and getting them approved by the doctors and nurses. After receiving their approval we had to print them and arrange for a logical way of stocking and tracking them.

Janet Guizzetti, vice president of personnel of a hospital in Denver, Colorado, arrived in God's perfect timing. Forms were no big deal to her. Together, we spent days making lists of forms and, following that, lists of our lists. We set up a temporary office in one of the vacant staff houses just to have a place to spread out our papers and work on forms. Since we didn't have commercial electricity we had to occasionally turn on the generator to keep our laptop batteries charged.

Janet enjoyed designing the forms, or at least she led me to believe so. She designed a method of categorizing each type of form and assigning it a stock number. After her departure from Yetebon, Janet continued to design forms and work with me on the categorization process by e-mail. After a few weeks I felt I had conquered the forms monster, thanks to her help.

Eventually we could see down the tunnel far enough to anticipate opening the hospital to the public. In May 2004, the Project Mercy head office in Addis Ababa began hiring the medical staff. Since Addis Ababa is much more centralized and accessible to professional medical people than remote Yetebon, we received curriculum vitae (CVs, or résumés) of applicants there. Thus, the doctors, nurses, technicians, druggists, etc., came through the Addis Ababa office; however, we filled the lower level jobs (such as guards, cleaners, gardeners, kitchen staff, and PHCAs) from the local population.

Dr. Kassaye Tilahun, a general practitioner and a very amiable, cooperative, and easy-to-love Christian believer, was appointed the medical director. He and I got along extremely well and remain very close friends. In many hospitals, doctors and the administration don't get along well, but that was no problem for Dr. Kassaye and me. Some of the other doctors were more problematic, but Dr. Kassaye and I usually could work our way through the sticky issues.

Our close friendship helped to avoid one particular potential area of conflict. In American hospitals, the top administrator (the CEO) is usually a business person trained in hospital administration. In Ethiopia, the top administrator almost always (although it is gradually changing) is a doctor. Marta and Deme initially appointed me as the administrator, desiring to follow the American pattern. However, this upset some of our doctors, who believed a doctor should be the administrator. Eventually those doctors wore Marta and Deme down and they reversed their opinion, appointing Dr. Kassaye as hospital administrator. Dr. Kassaye didn't want to be involved in all the non-medical issues and decisions, though—he simply wanted to practice medicine. So, in a very agreeable manner, we acted as sort of co-administrators, with never an argument over turf.

In May 2004 and the months following, Dr. Kassaye and I spent many hours in meetings regarding the upcoming opening of the hospital and how it should function once we began seeing patients. We both strongly agreed on a phased opening, beginning with seeing outpatients only. This also required that the laboratory, X-ray, and pharmacy be ready to go on Day One. A few weeks after the outpatient department and related functions opened, the emergency room would be brought online. Then we would open the medical ward for medical (e.g., malaria, HIV, tuberculosis, pneumonia) patients. Following that would be the pediatrics ward for the children. Next would be labor and delivery for handling gynecological cases and childbirth. And finally, after all those areas were functioning smoothly, we should open the operating rooms and the surgical ward. It seemed like a good plan.

Somewhat unfortunately, the Addis Ababa headquarters had already hired a gynecologist and a surgeon. They arrived at the hospital very eager to get started in their disciplines and didn't want to wait for phased openings. For a while, though, Dr. Kassaye and I prevailed and convinced them to be patient.

On September 15, 2004, we opened the hospital to the public with no announcement and no fanfare. Along with a prayer with Marta and Deme and the hospital staff, we simply told the guard he could tell passersby we were open for business. Four people came that day, but three had no money. The fourth, our first "real" patient, was a lady suffering renal (kidney) failure and had to be referred to a specialized hospital in Addis Ababa.

Marta and Deme determined that our hospital would accept no financial help from the federal or local governments of Ethiopia. If we did, we would be required to treat for free all patients that brought an authorizing document from the local government proclaiming that the patient was indigent. It is a real headache for hospitals that accept these papers, because eventually all patients end up being "indigent." Government hospitals are required to honor these papers, and it has become a huge burden for them, as they must accept these patients and treat them for free. By not accepting government funds, we were able to avoid this problem.

Sometimes it tore at our hearts to turn someone away who said they couldn't pay. We foreigners would never have been able to do so, but on the other hand we could never have afforded to treat all of those indigent patients, either. We left that job to our staff, who handled the situations in a culturally appropriate manner. Many times our reception room staff members explained to a patient that we could not accept his local government paper, and then out would come a big wad of cash, with the patient paying the required fees.

We kept our fees very low. It cost only 60 U.S. cents to see a doctor. The cost of a normal delivery of a baby was less than $4, and a Caesarean delivery was less than $25.

Only a few days after opening, a young boy and his sister showed up with severe cases of relapsing fever. This disease, caused by a borrelia bacteria transmitted by lice or ticks, can cause death in a short time if not treated immediately. These children, because of their distance from the hospital, were in grave condition by the time they arrived. Although our ER was not yet open, we quickly prepared it and gave them round-the-clock treatment. I remember being very impressed and somewhat frightened when Dr. Kassaye invited me to accompany him to the ER to treat the boy. With the child hooked up to a monitor, Dr. Kassaye told me he planned to inject medicine into the IV line, making the child's vital signs resemble those just preceding death. However, in a few minutes, after the medicine killed off the offending bacteria in the boy's system, he would recover and probably be fine.

I watched that scenario unfold and almost tore from the ER

when all the child's vital signs showed his bodily functions shutting down. I didn't want to see that little boy die right in front of my eyes. But Dr. Kassaye's prediction proved extremely accurate. Both the boy and his sister survived and went home healed. As a follow-up procedure we sent our sanitarian to fumigate their mud hut to eradicate the ticks. Many of their clothes and possessions had to be burned.

There was no turning back. Our emergency room had become operational much earlier than planned.

The biggest test of our phased opening plan came when a little three-year-old boy named Rahim came to the hospital with about four inches (ten centimeters) of his intestines hanging out of his rectum. Although three, he was so malnourished and sickly that he appeared to be only about eighteen months old. Rahim was an orphan, with only a slightly older sister to care for him. Some concerned neighbors carried him down the mountain to our hospital as a last resort after having no success with the traditional healer. Rahim was so near death that Dr. Kassaye and our surgeon, Dr. Berhanu Nega, estimated his chances of survival, even with surgery, as less than 5 percent, "probably nearer 1 percent."

I will never forget Dr. Berhanu pleading with me to allow them to operate. His heart-piercing logic was, "How can it hurt? This little boy is going to die anyway, so let's give him whatever small chance we can."

Dr. Berhanu had, by that time, been at the hospital for months and was anxious to get into the operating room. Practically every day we heard him exclaim, "I want to see blood."

As a businessman, I countered, "Dr. Berhanu, you know that our OR isn't ready. It would take a long time to set it up, clean it, and sterilize everything. Besides that, we have no one who can legally sign the consent form. And do you want our first surgery to result in a death?"

As I looked back on that incident, I realize I sounded like a bureaucrat, and I despise bureaucrats. I later regretted that response to Dr. Berhanu.

The doctors begged me to come and look at the little boy. When I saw him, my heart filled with compassion, and I told Dr. Berhanu, "If you can prepare the OR and the anesthesia machine, sterilize your instruments, and do all the other things necessary, you have my permission to operate."

The surgical team stormed into action, cleaning, scrubbing, disinfecting, and sterilizing the OR. They prepped Rahim, wheeled him into the OR, and placed him on the operating table. Many of the hospital staff prayed during the procedure. Later in the afternoon, Dr. Berhanu wrapped up the operation, and the nurses wheeled Rahim into our makeshift ICU. He had survived the surgery. In the evening, as I left the hospital, I checked, and he was still alive.

The following morning, upon entering the hospital, I expected to hear that the boy had expired during the night and that we now had a dead body to deal with. But I was wrong. The nurses excitedly told me that little Rahim had survived the night and was actually getting stronger. He became a celebrity and a mascot around the hospital. Everyone was so proud of him. And Dr. Berhanu had his wish—the operating rooms were also now open for business, months ahead of Dr. Kassaye's and my schedule. This meant the entire hospital now stood open for business, only just a couple of weeks after we started seeing patients.

Since little Rahim's family consisted of only a sister, Marta took him in as one of Project Mercy's orphans in the lower compound. He got stronger and stronger and soon was able to run and play with the other kids. One day while I was at the lower compound, I thought I saw Rahim fly past and called out, "Rahim, Rahim." But the child just ran past me. So, I muttered something like, "Well, that kid sure looks a lot like Rahim." The other children laughed and told me that he had renamed himself Abenezer.

No one knows where he came up with the name Abenezer, but that is now his name.

One day a young couple came in to Dr. Abdissa's examination room complaining they were unable to have babies. They had been married for a couple of years, and no children were forthcoming. As any gynecologist would, Dr. Abdissa asked them many probing questions, trying to determine their problem. He never expected to learn that their "problem" was a lack of education as to how babies are made and that they had never consummated their marriage.

Dr. Abdissa is a big man, but somewhat shy and introverted. With some degree of embarrassment he realized he needed to tell that married couple about the birds and the bees, which he proceeded to do. Afterwards when he told some of us about these unique patients, we broke out in uncontrollable laughter. I told Dr. Abdissa that he probably had the happiest patients in the world that day.

While at Project Mercy, no one ever asked me to explain how babies are made, but I was surprised to be asked to preach in our local church. One day the Project Mercy evangelist, Yohannes, handed me a small piece of paper written in Amharic. I studied it, looked at him inquisitively, and said, "If I'm reading this correctly you've scheduled me to preach in church two Sundays from now."

This notice really surprised me, since I have never had any training in preaching and merely considered myself a businessman called to administrative duties on the mission field.

With a big smile he confirmed, "That's correct. The church elders in their last meeting voted to add you to the preaching rotation."

"But you don't understand. I'm a hospital administrator, not a preacher. I'd be very uncomfortable doing that."

"Mr. Gary, please, it's the will of the church leaders that you preach. Your turn will come up only about every six weeks or so."

I couldn't convince Yohannes that I wasn't cut out for

preaching. Finally, I said, "It'll be in English, as I'm not that good in Amharic."

"That's okay; we'll get a translator for you."

So I prepared a sermon and found that Dr. Kassaye was going to be my translator. It worked well, but I felt uncomfortable preaching, especially through a translator. I secretly hoped the congregation would find my sermon so boring that they would withdraw their request for me to be in the rotation. Instead I received another small paper a few days later with my next preaching assignment. Again I preached in English. That continued for another turn or two.

In an attempt to relieve the awkwardness of preaching through a translator, I made a huge decision to try to one sermon in Amharic. I wrote out the entire sermon. For ten stressful days leading up to my Sunday turn I practiced my sermon every evening. My stress turned into Peggy's stress.

Now I knew I would really bore the congregation by mostly reading my sermon in Amharic. But to my amazement the Ethiopians loved it. They asked me never to preach in English again.

I replied, "But you have got to be so bored with my reading the sermon and all my mistakes and mispronunciations."

"We like it. We learn a lot from you."

So, until I left Yetebon I regularly took my turn for the Sunday sermon. I never got over the fear and anxiety. And Peggy dreaded my laboring over each sermon preparation whenever my turn came around.

But, today, many of our friends from Yetebon, when talking about me, never refer to me as the former hospital administrator. Instead, they remember me as the white man who preached in Amharic.

I could tell many stories of our next three years at Yetebon. But I could never adequately describe the multitude of close friendships we developed, the guests and volunteers we came to love, the trips we took, the bringing of electricity and telephone to Yetebon, our tiny but comfortable house, our neighbors, potlucks, and cookout bonfires, trips to Butajira, deaths, births, marriages, funerals, sorrows, joys, and all the other tremendous God-given experiences.

The four years spent in Yetebon may be the richest four years of our lives. As the only full-time white workers at the hospital, Peggy and I came to be respected as "Ethiopian" as any other person there.

CHAPTER 26

Something's Not Right

As supervisor of the metal-working shop for Project Mercy, Temesgin Obsa trained young men from the Yetebon community to skillfully make shelves, roof trusses, and gates in his shop. He also became a very good friend of mine. Whenever I needed something made from metal for the hospital, Temesgin saw to it that my request was completed as quickly as possible, often moving it to the top of the priority list.

He fell in love with Addis, a young lady who also worked at Project Mercy, training the women of the village in spinning cotton, basket weaving, and embroidery. Her students turned out impressive work, eagerly sought by foreign visitors to Yetebon.

Temesgin and Addis became engaged, announced their wedding day, and invited Peggy and me. As a matter of fact, they invited us to spend the entire day with them, starting with an early morning breakfast, all the way through to a formal dinner well into the evening.

Addis and her sister were married on the same day, but in different churches. Addis and Temesgin were married in an evangelical Christian church, and Addis' sister was married in an Orthodox Christian church, both churches located in Addis Ababa.

Early in the morning we went to Temesgin's house to begin the festivities. None of his three attendants knew how to tie a tie, so I had the honor of tying all three ties. We had breakfast while more and more guests arrived.

After an extended breakfast, Ethiopian tradition requires the groom to go to the bride's house and take her to the church. Upon arrival at the bride's home the large accompanying procession sings and dances and with good-natured chants warns the groom that he is not worthy to take the bride and should not be allowed to enter her house.

When we got to Addis' home, Peggy and I entered and saw both young ladies sitting together dressed in white. Tongue in cheek, I warned Temesgin to be sure to choose the right one. Following the visit to the bride's house, we went to the wedding ceremony at the church, then to the reception, and finally to the evening dinner. Peggy and I were ushered to place of honor on the stage along with the bride and groom. It was a blessed day, and we were very happy for Temesgin and Addis as they started their new home together.

Some time later, back at Yetebon, I saw Temesgin looking very sad. He had his Project Mercy release papers in his hand. When I asked him what was wrong, he told me that he and Addis had been terminated. When I asked why, he could only shrug his shoulders with tears in his eyes. I figured I must have not known my friend as well as I thought I did. He and Addis both must have done something really bad to be fired so abruptly. They moved back to Temesgin's hometown of Ziway. Little did we suspect then how interconnected our lives would become in just a few short years.

Over the next few months, we witnessed a number of other strange terminations—a couple of teachers, our hospital house-keeping supervisor, my hospital business manager (and right-hand man), a cement mason, and others. This seemed quite strange to me, because of those I knew well, none had done anything deserving of termination that I knew of.

We began to wonder if such a thing could ever happen to us.

Sometimes Deme and Marta briefly told us why they had to terminate someone. Their explanations seemed to make sense but didn't match up with our observations. We just chalked it up to cultural differences we didn't understand. For a while Peggy and I thought we were immune to termination because of the critical nature of our jobs at the hospital and because we were volunteers.

Then it started happening to us, although the impact didn't register until later. We asked Marta and Deme for meetings to discuss hospital issues, but they never could find time to meet with us. This forced me to make large, important decisions I would have preferred to consult with them about in order to keep the hospital running smoothly.

Marta and Deme had given us a small bedroom, along with a bathroom, with an outside entrance at their house in Addis Ababa. We felt very blessed by their generosity and enjoyed the freedom of having our personal quarters whenever we went to Addis Ababa for business or to resupply. Often they invited us to come into the main house to have breakfast with them. But, whenever the mealtime conversation turned to decisions or concerns regarding the hospital, they abruptly ran out of time to talk. Our frustration mounted as there never seemed to be time to consult with them on important issues.

Many volunteers from the U.S. (both individuals and teams) had trouble contacting Marta and Deme. Those volunteers learned to contact Peggy and me instead to find the answers to their questions about traveling to and volunteering at Yetebon. We regularly corresponded with potential volunteers regarding when to come, what to bring, and what to plan to do.

One team from a church in New Hampshire had a really difficult time getting any information from either the Project Mercy office in Ft. Wayne or the office in Addis Ababa. That church usually sent a very valuable work team to Yetebon each year. When they couldn't find the information they needed, they contacted me. I also tried to contact Marta and Deme to see what tools and supplies they should bring and what they should plan to do when in Yetebon. Finally, as the time drew very close for them to leave New Hampshire and with still no word forthcoming from Deme and Marta, I sent them a list of projects I had on my to-do list. Relieved to know what they would be doing in Yetebon, they brought tools and supplies for the projects I had suggested (put a new roof on the incinerator shed, start the diesel engine on a generator that had not turned over for years, etc.). They also brought a lot of supplies for the hospital—drugs, sutures, and other badly needed materials.

The Saturday they arrived I waited anxiously to meet the team. Over the years we had developed friendships with some of the team members, and they usually looked us up on arrival. At church the next morning we finally met the team. Our really good friends greeted us warmly, but some of the team seemed unusually cool and reserved toward us. One of the team members told us that Deme told them all the hospital supplies they brought should be locked up in a room at the lower compound and not be delivered to the hospital. He also told them that except for the two nurses on the team, no one would be working at the hospital. Instead they would be building cabinets for the orphanage.

This mention of the cabinet project surprised all the team members. Most felt quite disappointed. They said they really weren't woodworkers but rather were recruited for the projects I had written them about. Not knowing they were to build cabinets, they didn't bring tools or supplies for that kind of work.

At the end of the church service, I went to Deme and said, "Gashe [term of respect for an older person], I'm a little confused. I was expecting help with some projects at the hospital, but the team is telling me that they are going to be working in the lower compound."

Coldly looking me in the eyes, Deme told me, "Except for the two nurses, no one will be working at the hospital. They have other work to do."

Stunned, I responded, "Deme, there seems to be a different spirit between us. Can we talk about it?"

"I don't have time to talk now," he replied and turned to another guest. This was not the same Demeke Tekle-wold I had known and loved to this point.

On our walk back to our house I told Peggy of the conversation between Deme and me. She couldn't believe it. We thought and thought about what we could possibly have done to bring this about, but came up with nothing.

Determined to know how we had offended them, we called Marta and Deme and asked if we could talk. They told us if they saw any time open up in the future they would let us know.

After a couple of weeks had elapsed and having heard nothing, we wrote them a formal letter asking for an opportunity to discuss their change of heart toward us. As their brother and sister in Christ we wanted to apologize to them for any offense we may have caused, make any necessary restitution, and reconcile. We didn't want any hard feelings between us.

Eventually they called, saying they could meet with us the following Sunday afternoon in Addis Ababa. I explained I was scheduled to preach in the Emmanuel Church in Butajira that morning, but we would gladly go to Addis immediately after the service to meet them.

We drove the two and a half hours to Addis Ababa with heavy hearts, as again the Spirit prepared us for something unpleasant.

Upon arrival at their house we were ushered into the living room. Marta said Project Mercy board member Norm Whitney would be sitting in on the meeting. We weren't exactly excited about that, as we wanted a private talk with Marta and Deme, but we relented.

Except for Marta and Deme, Norm represented the first Project Mercy board member to visit Yetebon in our four years of service there. Even though he was in Yetebon for over two weeks, he had not taken even five minutes to meet us. It seemed quite strange that a board member would not be interested in getting to know the hospital administrator, considering the importance of the hospital to Project Mercy's ministry. We wondered how Norm could possibly know anything about our situation except for what he heard from Deme and Marta.

In what was one of the strangest conversations I have ever participated in, Marta and Deme kept referring to some unnamed things we had done. But we could never convince them to specify what those things were. They did allude to bad things we had said about them. We asked, "Why would we say bad things about an organization and people we love and for which we have each given four years of our lives?" We ached to know the specifics of the accusations against us.

Two hours later we had talked around, over, and through those things but never learned the nature of our sins. We apologized profusely in general but didn't know what we were apologizing for.

Norm didn't say a word during the entire conversation, except at the end he said twice, "I think it would be best if we parted ways."

Part ways!

Over what?

Marta and Deme suggested we think it over and get back to them with our decision. Then they suggested we pray together. For the first time in the fifty-eight years of my life I could not possibly pray. I had tears running down my cheeks, and there was no spirit of prayer in me.

We left and went to a guest house operated by our friends from the Danish Evangelical Mission. Neither of us slept a bit that night. So hurt, so crushed, so confused—we could uncover no explanation for what had just happened to us.

By Tuesday, Peggy and I had thoroughly discussed the situation, trying to guess what we might have done, even speculating on some far-fetched things. We determined that just as it had been for Temesgin, the teachers, my business manager, and the others, it was simply our time to go. Even though we had no idea where we could go or what we would do, the situation at Project Mercy appeared to be untenable for us.

We called Marta and Deme and agreed to meet at the Hilton Hotel the next day. Under very strained conditions we sat down together for tea and juice. We told them, based on the spirit between us that didn't seem reconcilable at the time, and based on Norm Whitney's statements that it would be best if we parted ways, we had decided we should leave Project Mercy.

Even though we were sure that was the decision they wanted, they dramatically got up and left us without touching their drinks. Peggy and I looked at each other stunned, paid the bill, and left, not really knowing where to go.

CHAPTER 27

God Has Another Job for Us to Do

By now the reader may be thinking, "Gary, really, you surely had some idea what the problem was." But we truly, truly didn't, and to this day we still don't. After those strange conversations with Deme and Marta, we began the deepest self-introspection of our lives.

Did God have something else He wanted us to do?

Was this a signal to go back to the U.S. and the secular world?

Should we go to another country as missionaries?

With this experience following that of Wycliffe/SIL, were we really cut out for this missionary life?

Frankly, we loved Ethiopia. After nearly seven years our hearts had become bound up with the people and the land. Our roots had sunk deep. We prayed fervently for God to show us clearly our next steps, but we prayed especially hard that He would direct us to something in Ethiopia.

Little did we know then that over the next couple of months we would hear God speak to us as clearly as if He were sitting right beside us. Peggy and I decided that before we just summarily packed up and left the country, we should look around for other opportunities in Ethiopia. The list of possibilities was not very long, as most organizations required certain qualifications we didn't have.

For example, joining the large mission organization SIM

required going back to the U.S. and working our way through their application process as we had done with Wycliffe. To work with another church denomination probably would bring on doctrinal issues that could cause problems with our membership in the Apostolic Christian Church.

Peggy and I visited organizations such as Samaritan's Purse and USAID. We also talked with our friends at other mission organizations, but we didn't feel like we uncovered any potential at any of those places.

Esayas Sutuma, a lab technician who worked at the Project Mercy Hospital, became one of our especially close friends at Yetebon. After a while he left that hospital and joined the Korean Hospital (Myungsung Christian Medical Center) in Addis Ababa. When he heard we were leaving Project Mercy, he expressed his sadness and his concern that we might leave Ethiopia for good.

He invited us to visit him at the Korean Hospital, and we gladly accepted. It didn't take long to tour the lab, so he also took the time to show us the entire hospital. After we finished the hospital tour he said, "Let's see if Mr. Moon is in; I'd like to have you meet him."

Mr. Hong Ryang Moon (known as "Mr. Moon" or simply "Moon"), the Korean administrator of the hospital, was in his office and graciously invited us to come in. We shared experiences, especially regarding hospital administration, for about twenty minutes, and then Peggy and I left. I clearly recall saying to Peggy as we walked out of the Korean Hospital, "Well, it certainly seems there isn't anything for us to do here."

What we didn't understand was that God was putting puzzle pieces in place for us. We have learned through our experiences in Ethiopia that we should never turn down an opportunity to establish a friendship, or at least a relationship, whenever the opportunity presents itself. Amazing is not an adequate word to describe how relationships established at one time or place become significant later under different circumstances.

The International Evangelical Church (IEC), the church we normally attended when we were in Addis Ababa, stages a bazaar on the last Saturday of each month. Peggy loves this bazaar, as it is the place where many Christian NGOs (Non-governmental Organizations) sell their wares. For sale are pottery, rugs, woven goods, vegetables, Ethiopian jewelry, hand-made greeting cards, leather goods, spices, and many other things. If we are in Addis on the day of bazaar, Peggy makes it her priority to attend. After the first few times I went to the bazaar I tried to avoid it if at all possible; however, sometimes, if we were going to do something together afterwards, it was simply unavoidable.

On the days I accompanied Peggy to the bazaar I immediately went to the little snack shop and had a cup of coffee. Since the coffee room is always crowded, the patrons usually have to share tables with strangers or people they normally wouldn't drink coffee with. One particular bazaar Saturday I shared a table in the coffee room with Ruth Kennedy, a long-time friend of ours. Ruth, a Scottish midwife, became the "right-hand woman" to the founder and head of the Fistula Hospital, Dr. Catherine Hamlin.

Dr. Hamlin and her late husband, Dr. Reginald Hamlin, had started the Fistula Hospital in the early 1960s to treat young girls who had developed fistulas during childbirth. A fistula is a hole between two organs in the body, and in the cases of these young girls, it is usually between the birth canal and the bladder or the birth canal and the bowel.

In Ethiopia, especially in the countryside, young girls as young as eleven or twelve are often married off to older men. They become pregnant, and when it comes time to give birth, their little bodies simply are not big enough or mature enough to allow the baby to be born. After a long period of labor—potentially days—the baby's body, which is struggling to be born, tears a hole between the mother's birth canal and the bladder or the bowel, and the baby dies. The girl becomes incontinent. Her husband often divorces her. She returns to her family and they banish her to a hut away from the rest of the family because of her offensive smells and leaking urine or feces. She lies in her hut, her muscles atrophy, and she loses all hope for her future.

The Hamlins started the Fistula Hospital to repair the girls' fistulas at no charge. Most of the time the girls, after a full recovery, go back to their villages, get remarried, and have healthy babies.

We became acquainted with Ruth through Dr. Andrew Browning, an Australian gynecologist stationed at the Fistula Hospital, who was in Amharic language school with Peggy and me when we first arrived in Ethiopia. We became close friends with him and often visited him at his hospital, taking visitors along for tours. No one ever comes away from that hospital without being touched deeply by the dedication of the staff and the amazing stories of the girls. Many of the girls struggled hard and sacrificed dearly to get to Addis Ababa for that one ray of hope of receiving treatment for their incapacitating condition and family ostracism.

So when Ruth and I met in the coffee room at the bazaar we started off with the normal greetings and pleasantries. When she heard we were leaving the Project Mercy Hospital, she became very interested and said she would call me. She did call, and she told me she wanted me to come to the Fistula Hospital to meet the CEO, Mark Bennett.

We went to see Mark and had a very good meeting. Mark, a pleasant, easygoing Australian, explained to me his dire need for administrative help. Attracting a volunteer hospital administrator with experience in Ethiopia would be an answer to his prayers. We discussed potential arrangements and opportunities for Peggy and me. We all decided to pray about it and get back together again. In the meantime he said he would talk to Dr. Hamlin, the board of directors, and the other interested parties.

We met a couple more times, including our final meeting on the day we returned to the U.S. for our 2007 vacation. He told me that both Dr. Hamlin and the board of directors had approved our working at the Fistula Hospital, and he was looking forward to having me working alongside him. He said only a meeting with the management of the hospital remained, but that usually was a "rubber-stamp" approval. Our spirits soared as we left the Fistula Hospital prior to going to the airport later that day to fly to Chicago.

Mark told me that even though it looked like a sure thing, we could not publicly announce our plans to join the Fistula Hospital until after the management meeting. He promised to e-mail me just as soon as it happened. It felt good to quickly find meaningful positions where we were badly needed and would truly be serving the poorest of the poor.

During our six-week visit to the U.S., we told our friends and supporters of our plans to leave Project Mercy and that, going forward, we would most likely be working at the Fistula Hospital. Telling others about our transition made it appear so seamless. The sting of our departure from Project Mercy remained but was, thankfully, receding into the background.

Even though we didn't have final confirmation of our move to the Fistula Hospital, we owed it to our financial supporters to let them know what was happening. Since we felt God wanted us to continue as financially supported missionaries, we needed to find a new organization to process our donor's gifts. We had already asked our supporters back in 2003 to change from sending their checks to Wycliffe Bible Translators to sending them to Project Mercy. Now that we were leaving Project Mercy, where could we tell them to send their money? The Fistula Hospital is an Australian corporation, and we didn't feel that many of our supporters would be willing to send their money to Australia. In addition, they would not get a receipt for a charitable tax deduction for their United States income tax returns.

One day it dawned upon me that there must be a number of

501(c)(3) corporations that could receive our funds and issue receipts that would qualify for the charitable tax deduction. The term 501(c)(3) refers to a section of the United States Internal Revenue Code that allows qualifying organizations to receive funds tax-free and to issue receipts allowing the donor to deduct the amount of the gift from his taxable income.

I poked around a little and found several organizations that would be glad to do that for us. Some of them agreed to not assess an administrative fee on the funds that would flow through their organizations. We visited with several of these organizations and weighed the pros and cons of each. In the end we decided upon Loving Shepherd Ministries of Bluffton, Indiana. Its president, Ed Schwartz, is a good friend of ours, a man with the very responsible position of eldership over the largest church in our denomination. He also is a strong advocate of our missionary work.

Partnering with Loving Shepherd greatly blessed us. Going forward, we felt comfortable knowing that if God nudged us in a different direction, we would not have to ask our supporters to send money to a different address. And, in the transition from Project Mercy to Loving Shepherd, I don't think we lost a single financial supporter. This vote of confidence humbled Peggy and me as we clearly saw that our group of supporters believed strongly enough in our ministry to remain faithful to us.

With the issue of our finances settled, and one week left in our stay in Illinois, only one major item remained—that final, confirming e-mail from Mark Bennett. Because we had not yet received it, we still could not tell anyone officially of our intentions to work at the Fistula Hospital. It also meant that we couldn't notify anyone of our change of address for sending in our financial support. So I wrote to Mark and Ruth asking the status of our situation, reminding them of our quickly approaching return to Ethiopia.

The next morning I got up early, as usual, to go out and exercise by walking and running around our Bloomington neighborhood. Before I left the house I checked e-mail.

I was stunned!

My inbox contained e-mails from both Ruth and Mark, stating that the management committee had met and decided to deny our working at the Fistula Hospital! They offered two reasons for this decision. First, Mark had not abided by the hospital's required protocol of advertising for candidates for a job opening. He had created the administrative job just for me. Secondly, since the Fistula Hospital worked with Project Mercy from time to time, our separation from Project Mercy on such uncertain terms could make for difficult relations between the two organizations in the future.

I couldn't believe it!

Now what?

We had told many people of our plans to work at the Fistula Hospital. It had felt so reassuring to know we had important and eagerly anticipated positions to return to Ethiopia for.

I went out for my exercise full of anger, humiliated, upset, and disappointed to the core.

I turned my anger toward God. "How could You do this to me? What is the meaning of this? Here I am, off serving You in Ethiopia as I thought You had called me, and now You pull the rug from under my feet. What can we possibly tell our family and friends? We have nothing, nothing, nothing to go to Ethiopia for. If You didn't mean for us to go back to Ethiopia or to the Fistula Hospital, why did You string us along until now, when our bags are nearly packed? This is humiliating! Would You please tell me what You have in mind?"

I lost track of time and distance. I walked. I ran. I shouted. I had so much anger and frustration to release. I have no idea how long I was gone from home; nor could I possibly have retraced my steps. I determined not to go back home until I settled down. I couldn't face Peggy and my family in my out-of-control state.

As my walking and running continued and some semblance of calm returned, I started feeling bad about yelling at and questioning God that way. After all, He is God, and I am, in comparison, a dust ball (or less). My heart felt that I should apologize to Him, but my mind wasn't ready. Besides, I reasoned to myself, look at how He's treating me. I need an explanation.

Some weeks later, while reading Psalms, I found comfort in the fact that David (who was a man after God's own heart) had done the same thing. David seemed to have no hesitance about crying out to God, questioning God, and complaining to God. He is God. He is almighty. He can take it. He wants us to tell Him our feelings. He wants us to express our emotions. I am confident that He would prefer to have us come to Him charged with raw emotion than with a prepackaged, canned, and memorized prayer.

But all that philosophizing didn't help me that fateful day. When David wrote in his songs (psalms) that he was in the pit, he was also describing where I was that day. There we were, David and I, snuggled together down there in the mire. What a long, miserable day stared me in the face with no relief in sight in any direction!

I wondered if we should cancel our flight back to Ethiopia and start looking for a secular job in the U.S. Or should we seek out another mission opportunity? Who do we talk to? Where do we start? Should we simply go back to Ethiopia and pack up our stuff and bring it back to our home in Illinois and see what happens?

I finally made it through the day and a long, fitful night. The next morning I woke up early again to do my trek around the neighborhood. Once again I checked e-mail before I went out.

I could not believe my eyes! I found a completely unexpected e-mail from Mr. Moon at the Korean Hospital. Since I think his Korean-English is so genuinely heartfelt, I am reproducing his message here, exactly as he wrote it:

Dear Gary !

Believe you have been enjoying enough rest with your family so far.

It was our great pleasure to see your couple and share our vision with you before your departure.

We have been praying on the way of our co-working in our hospital and we would like invite you as a CIO/Chief Information Officer whose job is

1. All the works related to the information, advertisement
2. International collaboration including training program, fundraising, etc.
3. Planning and implementation of projects

Please consider above suggestion seriously and let us know your opinion.

Also please don't hesitate to ask further question, if you have.

While would you mind sending your C/V again with your church background as I mislayed it somewhere and I can't find it?

Looking forward to your encourageous response.

God bless you

Best regards/Moon

Exactly twenty-four hours later I climbed out of the slimy pit and onto the fluffy clouds.

Someone needed me! God had another position for us. This invitation, so entirely out of the blue, shook me to my foundations. We had not spent but twenty minutes in Mr. Moon's office, never once discussing the possibility of working at the Korean Hospital. The closest we came to the subject was telling Mr. Moon of our plans to leave the Project Mercy Hospital and that we didn't know

God's direction for our future. I did give him my résumé, as one would a business card, as an introductory formality, since I had extras with me.

After reading his e-mail that morning I ran like a deer. I felt like maybe I could fly. We had a purpose; our lives had meaning. The Holy Spirit was working in Mr. Moon. Later, when I asked him what prompted him to write the invitation e-mail, he said he couldn't exactly say what had caused him to do so. He had no idea how we would respond or if we were even interested. It is not typical in Korean culture to invite unknown non-Koreans to work with them. Over the next year and a half of working at the Korean Hospital, we learned how truly unusual that invitation was.

It seemed quite strange for us, in a way, to think of working with the Koreans, and we really didn't understand how we would fit in. But we did know there was nothing clearer on earth that day than God's message for us. A few months later we discovered the real reason God wanted us at that hospital.

CHAPTER 28

Myungsung Christian Medical Center

Once we received, and accepted, our invitation to work at the Korean Hospital, we eagerly packed and headed back to Ethiopia with a purpose in our lives and a spring in our step. Because we didn't have a home in Addis, we reserved a room at the Danish Evangelical Mission guest house, the same place we had gone after our fateful meeting with Marta and Deme.

Surprising, but graciously, Marta and Deme had allowed us to leave our things in our Yetebon house during our U.S. vacation. However, arriving just one month prior to the Ethiopian Year 2000, we received notice from them to immediately remove our things from our former rural home.

In Ethiopia everything dealing with time is different from what the rest of the world considers normal. The country is on "biblical time," making it six hours different from the rest of the world. For example, the Ethiopian day begins at what we in the U. S. call 6:00 a.m., which Ethiopia calls the twelfth hour. In the Bible where it says, "Now Peter and John went up together into the temple at the hour of prayer, being the ninth hour" (Acts 3:1 KJV), the "ninth hour" is 3:00 p.m. for most of the world, but in Ethiopia it is also the ninth hour (calculated from 6:00 a.m., or the twelfth hour).

With thirteen months in its calendar—twelve of exactly thirty days each and one of five or six days—a popular Ethiopian tourism jingle touts its "thirteen months of sunshine." And Ethiopia uses the Julian calendar, about seven years and nine months behind the Gregorian calendar, which most of the rest of the world uses.

The Ethiopian New Year's Day is September 11. Thus, the western world's September 11, 2007, was the first day of the first month of 2000 in Ethiopia and was therefore the beginning of the new millennium (or Y2K, as we had called it in the West nearly eight years before).

As an aside, fortunately the rest of the world had cleared the way for the Ethiopian Y2K, as we experienced no frightening predictions of millennium meltdown due to our calendars turning over to the year 2000. Or was it due to the fact that electronic technology had not yet infiltrated all aspects of Ethiopian lives?

There was a great anticipation that many Ethiopians from the diaspora would return to celebrate the new millennium and then stay for a long time visiting relatives and friends while enjoying the country of their heritage. Because of that perception, house rents skyrocketed, as every Ethiopian wanted to rent out his house to the millennium visitors and make lots of quick money. We found all available housing in the process of being readied for this anticipated large influx of visitors. People told us about their landlords doubling their house rents overnight. Some of our Ethiopian friends even planned to move out of their houses into their service quarters (most Ethiopian families have several rooms in a small building outside the main house, often used as rooms for house workers and guards) so the main house could be rented to the millennium guests.

Needless to say, this made for a rough housing market as we again found ourselves searching for a home in Addis Ababa. Initially, we thought we were in luck and would be able to move into the nice guest house on the Korean Hospital property. Mr. Moon offered us a two-bedroom apartment rent-free in return for volunteering at the hospital. Eager to avoid another daunting house-hunting experience and paying rent, our enthusiasm waned as we toured the one tiny vacant apartment.

When we walked into the kitchen, Peggy gave me "the look" that there was no way we would live in that place. Her kitchen is her castle and must meet at least her basic standards. In our small Yetebon kitchen Peggy could stand in one spot and touch the sink, stove, and refrigerator. In the Korean guest house apartment, there wasn't even a stove, only a cook plate. The kitchen had barely room to walk into. When Peggy graciously declined the offer of a "free" apartment, Mr. Moon replied, "I guess Koreans are used to living in a smaller space than Americans are."

In Ethiopia there is no such thing as a realtor who has access to all available houses in the city. We knew from previous experience that we would have to hire a delala (agent) to help us find a house. Finding a good delala is a real challenge. If I tell the delala the maximum amount of rent I can pay is 7,000 birr per month (at the time of this writing approximately $600 U.S.), I know I will never see a 6,000 or 7,000 birr house. I will see only houses with rents of 8,000 birr and up. He will try to convince me that his negotiating skills will bring the price down to 7,000 birr.

Delalas network aggressively with each other using their mobile phones. The delala may tell me in the morning he has two houses to show us. As we head off to those houses, he is networking with his delala buddies. We may end up spending all day looking at houses, usually fruitlessly and outside the previously established price range. Sometimes we found ourselves with as many as four delalas in the back seat of our car, all frantically working their phones. And all were anticipating a piece of the commission pie.

Peggy and I asked Mr. Moon for a couple of weeks off to find a new home and move our goods in from Yetebon. The deadline Marta and Deme set for us to evacuate our Yetebon house added to the pressure and stress. In spite of the inflated rental rates due to the millennium frenzy, we found a nice house about seven kilometers (four miles) from the Korean Hospital. Thankfully the Lord provided us this home just ahead of the deadline. We immediately moved all our things to Addis with a Project Mercy Isuzu straight truck in the same manner we had taken those same household goods out to the Project Mercy site four years before.

Mr. Moon warmly welcomed us to the hospital. We discussed our roles and other administrative details and immediately started our work. Peggy and I committed to Mr. Moon to work at the Korean Hospital for two years.

The Korean Hospital is officially known as Myungsung Christian Medical Center, or MCM, for short. The Myungsung Presbyterian Church of Seoul, South Korea, built MCM as an outreach of its 100,000-strong membership. Although Ethiopia is its primary focus, the church supports missionaries all over the world.

When the senior pastor of the Myungsung Church visited Ethiopia in 1993, the prime minister implored him to do some development work for the Ethiopians, suggesting something along the line of health care. The pastor took this message back to Korea, and the congregation decided to build a state-of-the-art hospital.

Interestingly, although somewhat hard to fathom today, Ethiopia sent 6,000 troops to help South Korea during the Korean War. The South Koreans freely admit that one of the primary reasons they want to help Ethiopia is because the Ethiopians helped them in their time of need.

The Ethiopian government donated nine hectares (twenty-two acres) of prime property. The hospital construction commenced in 1998, and the hospital opened on November 25, 2004 (just over two months after we had opened the Yetebon hospital on September 15, 2004). As administrator of the Project Mercy Hospital, I had received invitations for Peggy and me to attend MCM's dedication, never suspecting in the least that we would be working there someday. Since that beginning, MCM has come to be recognized as the best general hospital in Ethiopia.

When we told Mr. Moon that Peggy was a dietitian (he hadn't inquired about her training previously), his voice quivered, and we choked up when he told us they had been praying for a dietitian for several years. Because of her degree in dietetics and her hospital experience, Peggy fit naturally into her role as food service director, with responsibility for the kitchen, cafeteria, and the patients' meals.

Peggy has high standards, so she had a lot of work ahead of her to bring the kitchen up to her expectations. She prepared documents to track food inventory and prices, and she regularly went shopping with the hospital driver to purchase the large quantities of food necessary to keep the kitchen running. Many staff members and patients benefited from the classes she taught on nutrition, including the women enrolled in the prenatal classes offered by the nursing office.

As for me, Mr. Moon initially placed me in charge of what I called the "three Ps"—personnel, planning, and publicity—and gave me an office on the second floor of the hospital. It seemed, though, every week he expanded those responsibilities. After I began to understand how busy he was with so many responsibilities, I decided it must have been on one of those days of frustration and desperation that he had turned to me for help, even though I wasn't Korean and was an unknown entity.

Mr. Moon and I immediately gained a great deal of respect for each other. Almost any time he left the hospital to call on another business or government official, he asked me to go along. He requested that I sit in on almost every meeting because of his lack of confidence in his English. Many days I found myself translating English to English; i.e., from Korean-English to Ethiopian-English and back again. The Ethiopians and Koreans often found it difficult to understand each other's English. As the native English speaker, I understood what each of them wanted to say and then repeated it clearly in American-English to the other party.

My responsibilities continued to increase and, along with that, so did my stress level. After a few months, Mr. Moon decided to vacate his office to make room for the pediatrics out-patient clinic. A new prefab building was built outside the main hospital building to house the laundry and the equipment maintenance office and workshop. Mr. Moon wanted to move his office to a portion of the former laundry area. He also wanted my staff and me to move to a large room just outside his new office. All of that was very agreeable to me.

One day soon after asking my staff and me to join him on the first floor upon completion of the remodeling, Mr. Moon surprised me with a visit to my upstairs office.

He said, "Gary, I would like for you to move into my new office with me."

Quite surprised, I responded that I didn't know how that would work. So we went together down to the former laundry area. Pointing to the proposed outline of his new office, he explained, "See, my desk will be here, and yours will be right beside mine," pointing to areas about one meter apart.

"But what about Hirut [his secretary]? You've always had her in your office with you."

"I don't want that any longer. She will be just outside our door with Rosa [my secretary]."

Interestingly, Koreans like small apartments but they prefer big offices. In our proposed office were to be two sofas, a small table, a television, a big boom box, and several cabinets and book-cases for storage. He had allowed room for his secretary's desk, but he now indicated he preferred to have me there.

I reiterated, "I don't think that plan will work. There won't be privacy for either of us. When I am on the phone, it will disturb your work. If either of us needs to have a private conversation, the other will have to leave the office. You will have to listen to all my meetings, and I will have to listen to yours."

But the real reason for my hesitance was that it simply went against the grain of my culture. This concept would never fly in America, and I was very uncomfortable sitting only a few feet away from the CEO of the hospital. It almost made us appear to be equals.

I continued, "I will be very content sitting out there in the big room with my staff. I will be very close every time you need me."

"No, Gary, I want you in here. I'm not worried about status. Please go along with me on this."

Not knowing what else to say, to buy time I responded, "Let me see what Peggy says."

"Okay, but I insist we share this office."

I went to Peggy and told her what Mr. Moon was proposing and that I was quite uncomfortable with his proposed arrangement. "It just simply doesn't feel right," I insisted.

She answered, "Well, if he is so insistent about your sharing the office, you probably should go along with it. Maybe it will help if you ask him for a partition between your two desks."

So I went back to Moon. "Okay, I'm willing to give it a try. However, can we have a partition right here between our desks?"

"Sure, that's a good idea. We'll put in a half-height partition. Good, I'm glad you agreed."

The partition, though, was never installed.

In spite of my reservations, the arrangement for the most part worked out quite well. Since we both usually sat in meetings together anyway, it actually proved quite convenient. Communication couldn't have been simpler, since we were able to turn to each other and talk.

Mr. Moon and I had so many things in common with each other that we ourselves were amazed. We were the same age, both born in 1948. We both earned bachelor's degrees in chemistry and had master's degrees. We had both served in the armed forces of our countries. In our previous lives, prior to becoming full-time missionaries, we each had worked as businessmen. Eventually we both found ourselves working as hospital administrators in Ethiopia with no prior hospital management training. We even were the same height and had the same color of gray in our hair.

In February 2008, Mr. Moon took his annual vacation back to Korea, leaving me in charge of the hospital. While there he underwent a colonoscopy. One day after he returned to Ethiopia he asked me to scoot over to his desk and look at some pictures. These weren't the vacation shots I expected to see. I was shocked to learn they were of his stomach and small intestine. Seeing my friend's insides in a color photograph was disconcerting, especially with him sitting right next to me. His doctor had sent him the results of his colonoscopy via those pictures, along with the news that they found an area of "precancerous tissue" at the junction of his stomach and small intestine.

I felt terrible for my friend but had no comprehension at that time how Mr. Moon's diagnosis would drastically affect my life. That incident was the first small step on the road to my understanding the real reason God wanted us to leave Project Mercy and join the Korean Hospital. Later it seemed prescient that Mr. Moon wanted to share his office with me. I didn't even have to move my desk—as the acting administrator I was already in the hospital administrator's office.

The doctor ordered Mr. Moon back to Korea immediately for surgery to remove the precancerous tissue. Mr. Moon submitted and quickly flew home. The surgeon removed two-thirds of his stomach. After that he started his cancer treatments and remained in the hospital for a long time. We kept in touch by e-mail and occasionally by phone. Mr. Moon always sounded positive about returning soon to Ethiopia.

In the meantime, the workload and accompanying stress that

had been transferred to me began to take a physical toll on me. I pushed myself very hard during the day and continued by working at home nights and weekends.

One day I noticed I couldn't make out the letters on the memo I was reading at my desk. I turned to my computer screen and couldn't make out the words there, either. I became very concerned, as my eyes simply would not focus. I walked to the room across the hall, where Peggy was at her desk.

"Peg, I need to go home."

"Why? What's wrong?"

"I can't see right. My eyes won't focus on the stuff I'm trying to read."

"What do you mean?"

"Well, when I try to read the papers on my desk or the computer screen, everything is blurry."

"If that's the case, this hospital is where you need to be, not at home."

"But I'm really tired. I just want to lie down. Where can I lie down and get any rest here?"

Peggy and a nurse took me to the doctors' overnight room and had me lie down there. Lying on the bed felt so good. But nurses and doctors interrupted my rest by coming and going, poking and probing, and asking me all kinds of questions. I just wanted to sleep.

After some lab tests and neurological examinations, they ordered a CT scan for me immediately after lunch. And finally they left me alone. I fell sound asleep and slept until lunchtime. My CT scan showed no problems. So, after a good rest in that bed, I got up, went back to my office, and worked until the end of the workday. I don't have any idea what went wrong, but I am sure that some neural circuit got overloaded. The sleep did wonders.

An incident occurred while I was administrator of the hospital in Mr. Moon's absence that is very significant to me. One day I got a phone call from a man saying he was calling from outside Ethiopia. His accent wasn't American, but I couldn't place where it was from. He told me that he and a couple of his colleagues would be meeting with me the following Monday at 1:30. It wasn't really a request, but rather more like an order. I agreed to meet them.

On Monday, I went out for lunch with one of our internal medicine doctors and came back at exactly 1:30 to find three people in my conference room. I went to my office and grabbed my notebook, and my secretary gave me "the look" indicating she was very concerned that I may have forgotten the meeting, since the guests acted so self-important.

The visitors introduced themselves as members of the United States Secret Service. The man who had called me was from the American embassy in South Africa, and his name was of Indian origin, which explained the non-American accent. They were very pleasantly surprised to find an American administrator of a Korean hospital in Ethiopia. They had checked out the hospitals in Addis Ababa and determined MCM was their choice. It would be the hospital that former president William J. Clinton would be brought to if he got sick or injured during his upcoming visit to Ethiopia. Not "Bill" Clinton, but "William J." Clinton. I told them I appreciated their confidence in us and assured them we would help in any way we could. President Clinton was scheduled to come to Ethiopia to review the work of his Clinton Foundation, which is doing a lot of good in the country.

Together we went through a very long and extensive question-naire inquiring about all the services we provided, the location of each, and every minute detail that could be relevant. They informed me, "Gary, we are required to inspect every detail of this hospital in anticipation that President Clinton may come here. If he comes, there will be Secret Service agents, as well as U.S. Marines and Ethiopian soldiers, stationed throughout the entire facility."

"You have my permission to check out everything. We are glad to cooperate. Just let me know whatever you need." After all, this was the United States Secret Service.

After intensively questioning me about our cardiac facilities, which were minimal, I understood their special concern about the former president's heart. In a feeble attempt to try to lighten things up a little, I commented, "Yeah, it's quite well known President Clinton likes his cheeseburgers." They didn't even crack a smile, further reinforcing the stereotype that the Secret Service has no sense of humor.

Located on the third floor ward was our VIP suite. It consisted of two rooms and contained a desk, TV, Internet connection, refrigerator, boom box, and microwave, in addition to a patient bed and medical facilities. I often wondered to myself why we had a VIP suite like this. It seemed that instead of encouraging the patient to rest, we were encouraging him to continue to work at the office.

The head of the Secret Service group informed me, "If President Clinton has to be admitted to this hospital we need your VIP suite for him. We will also need the patient room next to it for our command and control center. In addition to those, we need another room for press conferences."

I thought those were some pretty stiff demands, so I replied, "For the media you can use our chapel. Undoubtedly we can free up another nearby room for your command and control center. However, I truthfully cannot guarantee you the VIP suite. If, for example, the German ambassador would already be in there, we would not kick him out to make room for President Clinton. We will do the very best we can, however."

I don't think the Secret Service is used to being denied anything they ask for, but they seemed to understand. I didn't want any international incidents taking place while dignitaries squabbled over a room at our hospital.

Fortunately Mr. Clinton came to Ethiopia and left without needing to come to our hospital. Whew!

I continued to wonder if Mr. Moon would ever be able to return to Ethiopia. Over the phone he described to me his inability to keep food down and how he had lost a great deal of weight. March turned into April, which turned into May…and eventually July arrived. Peggy traveled back to the U.S. alone in mid-July, leaving me in Ethiopia to run the hospital.

Finally, in desperation, I e-mailed Mr. Moon that if he didn't return by the end of July, I would have to go back to the U.S. in spite of his not being back at the hospital. As a result of that correspondence, he said he would return on July 25 and I could go to the States a few days thereafter, after bringing him up to speed regarding what had happened over the intervening months since he left.

The calendar said July 25, and I eagerly anticipated Mr. Moon's arrival that day. Late in the morning I saw an East Asian man greeting my staff just outside my office. It wasn't until I saw my secretary stand up and greet him that I realized it was Mr. Moon. He had lost over thirty pounds (nearly fourteen kilograms) and had dyed his hair completely black. He later described how in Korean culture, when one part of the body gets weaker, they do something to make another part look stronger. Therefore, he dyed his hair to make himself look younger. Instead of sharing an office with a healthy looking sixty-year-old, I was sharing it now with a forty-year-old concentration camp survivor.

He looked so frail that I felt I could practically blow him over. His clothes hung loosely on his body because he was so skinny. Having only one-third of his original stomach, he had to eat small amounts of food many times a day. Due to his diminished energy level, Mr. Moon usually went back to his apartment in the afternoon for a nap. He rejoiced over every fraction of a kilogram of weight that he gained.

When Peggy and I returned to Ethiopia from our vacation, we found a somewhat stronger Mr. Moon. But he still had a long road of recovery ahead of him. He and I continued working side by side from our return in early September until November.

At that point, the home church back in Seoul decided that Mr. Moon was not capable of continuing in his duties as hospital administrator. They asked him to return to Korea and sent a new administrator, Mr. Kim Byung Soo, to take his place.

Mr. Kim had overseen the construction of the hospital in the late 1990s and early 2000s and thus was quite familiar with the hospital and Ethiopia. He said that I could stay or I could leave, whichever I wished to do. He never expressed a strong desire for my assistance as Mr. Moon had done. However, on the other hand, the invitation to stay and continue to serve at the hospital was genuine.

We had a lot of good friends at MCM and felt very fulfilled by our work and the things we had accomplished. Every day we met interesting people from all over the world. The challenges were huge, and my position would have been a dream job for many missionaries, and even non-missionaries. Peggy and I had comfortably settled into a nice house, had fulfilling employment, and worked with great co-workers of many nationalities.

But a capable Korean administrator was now in place. Even though our Korean, Norwegian, and Ethiopian co-workers expressed a great deal of appreciation for what Peggy and I did and encouraged us to stay, we felt the strong tug of God toward another "career." (The Korean Hospital had a large number of volunteers, including many nurses and doctors, from Norway, as well as financial supporters from that Scandinavian country. Almost all of the volunteers became our good friends.)

We had not quite made it to the end of our two-year commitment to Mr. Moon and the hospital. Peggy and I privately asked ourselves where the idea of a two-year commitment had come from. How could we possibly have known that two years would be just the amount of time needed to administratively cover the Korean Hospital for Mr. Moon? We reasoned that, without a doubt, God saw all of this unfolding and put each of us in our designated positions according to His plan.

We then understood that God had trained me as a hospital administrator and brought us to the Korean Hospital for Mr. Moon's time of need. During the tumultuous period of transitioning from Project Mercy, I could never have guessed this outcome. Perhaps the temporary diversion of seeking to volunteer at the Fistula Hospital had been my plan and not His. God used strong measures to steer me back to His path. I felt greatly humbled to clearly understand my position as an instrument in His hands during this period.

But that time of need had passed, and God seemed to whisper, "I've got another job for you to do."

CHAPTER 29

God Uses Relationships (I)

In January 2007, while we were still with Project Mercy, Ed Schwartz, president of Loving Shepherd Ministries, came to Ethiopia with Greg Isch, who was adopting a little Ethiopian boy. Greg's wife remained in Indiana to care for their other children, and in her place Greg brought Ed to help with the adoption.

Loving Shepherd Ministries encompasses several global outreaches, one of which is operating group homes for orphans. When they arrived at Yetebon to visit us, Ed met the many orphans being cared for by Project Mercy. They really touched his heart. He told us of his interest in establishing a group home in Ethiopia, too.

Nearly a year later, during our tenure at the Korean Hospital, we met Tsion Biru. Tsion, an Ethiopian woman approximately my age, was the hospital's receptionist. She seemed to know everyone, patients and employees alike. Due to her servant heart and the warmth and love she exuded, everyone called her "Mommy." Tsion seemed to be everywhere around the hospital, showing a visitor to the dentist's office or taking time to pray with a sick patient in the wards. She brought almost every foreigner or influential Ethiopian to my office to introduce them to me.

However, a conflict was brewing. One faction of Koreans felt she should sit at her reception desk and always be available to answer questions. Another faction said she should not merely point the way to the laboratory, for example, but actually escort the person there.

As human resources manager I regularly heard both sides of the conflict. One day one faction would come to my office complaining, "Tsion isn't at her desk. She's probably wandering around the hospital with a visitor. We need her to help take care of a patient, but she's nowhere to be found. Tell her to stay at the reception desk."

The next day the other faction would appear. "Tsion is simply sitting at her desk. She should be escorting the patients and visitors to where they want to go. Why is she just sitting there doing nothing? She needs to provide the personal touch in helping people find what they need in this hospital."

Following that, Tsion would show up in my office, nearly in tears and distressed. "Gary, one day I am scolded for sitting at my desk. The next day someone else yells at me for moving around. I can't seem to please anybody. What should I do?"

Upon investigating the situation, I discovered there was confusion over which department Tsion reported to. The nursing department thought she reported to nursing since they provided the bulk of hands-on patient care; the outpatient department thought she reported to them since she primarily served outpatients and that's where her desk was located; and medical records thought she reported to them because when the hospital originally opened with a much smaller staff, they were responsible for the receptionist.

After watching this ping-pong volley for a couple of weeks and getting my fill of the bickering, I announced one day, "Effective immediately the receptionist reports directly to the human resources manager. If anyone has a problem with Tsion's job performance they should report it to me and not talk to her or anyone else about it." Fortunately, that calmed the storm.

Some time after that, Tsion confided to Peggy that she wished she didn't have to work at the hospital at all. The desire of her heart was to take in orphan children and care for them. She already cared for two young orphans in her home, and she helped financially support several others.

When Peggy discovered this about Tsion, she probed deeper. Recalling Ed Schwartz's desire to build a group home in Ethiopia, Peggy asked Tsion if she knew a place available for Ed to construct such a home. Tsion immediately volunteered that she and her husband, Eshetu, would gladly give up their service quarters as a place to build a home for orphan kids. Their service quarters was a ramshackle building made of eucalyptus poles covered by mud, painted and covered by a rusting corrugated tin roof.

It turned out (isn't God amazing?) that Eshetu and Tsion's son, Yonas, is an architect. Peggy and I spent many hours with Yonas trying to squeeze a group home for eight children onto the same building footprint as Tsion's service quarters. If the area of the new building were no larger than the service quarters that were to be torn down, no permission from the local government was needed. Enlarging the building would mean beginning a long bureaucratic process to secure a building permit.

After Loving Shepherd agreed to sponsor the group home, we immediately started the work. Under the daily supervision of Eshetu, a retired government worker, the construction crew quickly demolished the old building and hauled away the debris. Construction of a beautiful, modern, cement-block building moved steadily along. Peggy went with Tsion, Eshetu, and Yonas to select the paint colors, fixtures, tile, furniture, and cabinets. After a couple of months we opened an impressive new home for orphan kids.

Tsion resigned from MCM and today lives out her dream of taking care of children who have no parents. She loves the kids and invests deeply in their spiritual, educational, and physical welfare. She teaches her children from an early age to read the Bible and expound on it. They memorize songs. Sincere prayer has become deeply entrenched in their lives, and Tsion has taught them to eagerly expect answers to those prayers.

They have assigned tasks that must be done every day. Each evening and on Saturday they complete designated hours of homework, computer training, sports, and free time. On Sunday mornings they pass out tracts in the taxi while traveling to church. Tsion is training her children to be responsible and productive citizens of Ethiopia and to be great advocates for the Kingdom of God.

The construction and operation of the group home met all of Ed's expectations, and he committed to building another group home for orphans in Ethiopia; however, he wanted it to be out in the countryside, where his heart had originally been attracted and where more space would be available.

CHAPTER 30

God Uses Relationships (II)

In the meantime, and unknown to us, God had other relationship tools in His heavenly toolbox that He planned to use to shape our future.

After my friend Temesgin left Project Mercy, he moved back to his hometown of Ziway, where he again took up his metal-working trade. Ziway is a rural town (population 45,000) approximately 160 kilometers (100 miles) south of Addis Ababa. Temesgin attended the Ziway Meserete Kristos Church (MKC), affiliated with the Mennonite Church in America. That congregation elected him to its board of elders.

Temesgin and I talked to each other by phone once or twice a year over the intervening years but rarely saw each other in person. In the spring of 2008, while Peggy and I were fully occupied at the Korean Hospital, Temesgin called to arrange a visit to our home in Addis Ababa. Since Mr. Moon was in Korea recuperating from his surgery, I had the full weight of running the hospital on my shoulders at that time. I was not looking for any more projects to take on.

When Temesgin came to our house he brought an invitation from the board of elders of the Ziway MKC for us to visit Ziway on June 6. He informed us that the elders of the church had been praying about us for a long time. It seems Temesgin had relayed to them the possibility that Peggy and I might be willing to help bring to fruition their vision for their church and community.

The elders wanted us to partner with them through development of a school, a home for abused girls, an orphanage, or any other institution that would help the disadvantaged people of Ziway. Temesgin told us that the elders possessed a strong vision, which they hoped we would also catch. He promised that if we moved to Ziway to help, the church had free land that they would give us, and they could provide a lot of inexpensive labor. However, he said they didn't have the necessary administrative skills and funding to achieve their goals.

Temesgin, having known me well from our time together at Yetebon and through observing me at the Korean Hospital, believed I was the person to provide the administrative capability they lacked. He and the other elders prayed that Peggy and I would be motivated to move to Ziway and start an integrated rural development project based on the pattern of Project Mercy.

We reminded Temesgin of our busy schedules but told him we were willing visit Ziway in June.

In my journal, at the conclusion of describing our conversation that day with Temesgin, I wrote, "What is God doing with us?" Long before knowing how the situation with Mr. Moon and the Korean Hospital would turn out, I wondered if God had already begun to plant in our hearts our next assignment. After all, we had committed to Mr. Moon only two years to work at the Korean Hospital.

On the appointed day we drove three hours south to Ziway, a slightly longer distance from Addis Ababa than Yetebon was. We met up with Temesgin, and he went with us to the MKC compound. As we entered he showed us the new church building under construction. We walked around behind it, and immediately Peggy and I stopped, dumbstruck. All 270 students who attended the MKC school stood in rows, dressed in their school uniforms, to greet us. One very cute little girl and boy couple, dressed in white Ethiopian national clothes, presented us with roses. Several students held up "Welcome" signs, and they all sang songs for us, in both Amharic and English. That warm and unexpected greeting touched Peggy and me deeply. We felt an instant bond with the church and its school.

Following a tour of the schoolrooms and after meeting the teachers, we found ourselves in the smallest, dingiest, most "bare-bones" church elder meeting room that one will find anywhere. After the elders explained the background behind their inviting us, the vision of the church, and some demographics of the community, I asked them to rank the top priorities of their vision. They gave us this list:

1. Build a bridge over a river to allow access to the village of Bochessa for evangelism.
2. Expand their school.
3. Assist with evangelism of surrounding communities.
4. Train their teachers and pastors.
5. Finish the construction of their church (at that time the cement block walls were up, but nothing had been started on the roof).

The priority order of their list surprised me. I was amazed that, even though the unfinished church building loomed just outside their door and its construction had been underway for seven years, finishing it was not their number-one priority. That their vision for serving others outweighed completing their own church impressed me.

The elders emphasized their access to free land, the availability of inexpensive manual labor, and their access to materials such as sand and gravel. They also claimed to have a lot of influence with local government officials, community leaders, and development officials.

Following their portion of the agenda, Peggy and I shared with them the vision Ed Schwartz had for building another group home out in the countryside of Ethiopia. This news encouraged the elders, and they eagerly agreed to support his vision and work together in any way they possibly could.

We e-mailed Ed about this opportunity immediately upon our return to Addis Ababa. Several factors piqued his interest, especially the availability of free land and the commitment to physically help construct a group home for orphans.

Buoyed by Ed's interest we returned to Ziway later in the year to visit Bochessa with the leaders of the Meserete Kristos Church to see the available land. With huge Lake Ziway on one side and the Bochessa River on the other, the poor village of Bochessa is essentially cut off from commerce, schools, medical care, and transportation. Part of MKC's vision, as laid out to Peggy and me, was to evangelize that strongly Muslim and Orthodox area with the gospel of Jesus Christ. Since communication and transportation problems make Bochessa very difficult to reach, the elders listed as their highest priority the building of a bridge over the Bochessa River. Once transportation of people and building materials was facilitated by a bridge, the MKC wanted to build a church, a school, a small clinic, and an orphanage in the village. By demonstrating the love of Jesus by executing these kinds of projects, the elders felt this would be a way to penetrate the hearts of the people of Bochessa with the gospel message.

Armed with a GPS apparatus Ed had sent me and my digital camera, we set out to investigate the three properties the Bochessa villagers offered us. After I sent him the GPS coordinates, Ed planned to use a program such as Google Earth to see their exact locations. Combined with digital photos sent by e-mail, he would have a good idea of the pros and cons of each available site.

We visited Bochessa prior to the rainy season, so the river was not flowing as high as it does at its peak. We were able to cross part of the way on huge stepping stones. In the deepest area the residents had built a rickety, slippery bridge of eucalyptus poles nailed across several long logs spanning the gap. Going back and forth to Ziway for the Bochessa villagers meant negotiating this dangerous bridge each way. If they had any donkeys, sheep, or horses accompanying them, or if they had heavy loads, they had to wade through the deep part of the river. During the rainy season when the water level was too high for the makeshift bridge, they had to hire a boat to ferry them across.

Crossing the river was dangerous and inconvenient any time of year. Tragedies like people being swept away by the stream and drowning or students dropping their books and school supplies into the muddy water regularly occurred while they negotiated the hazardous river crossing.

After crossing the river and entering the village area of Bochessa, we walked about six miles, looking at all three properties the village leaders were willing to give us. Once we saw them all, we met with the leaders for a long time at the village "meeting hall," which actually was a grassy spot under a large acacia tree in the "village square"—an open area surrounded by a mosque, mill, and several ramshackle mud buildings that had seen better days. A clinic building also stood on the "square," but we learned that its doors were usually closed because it rarely had any medicine or medical supplies.

When we returned to Addis Ababa we sent our report, including photographs and GPS coordinates, to Ed. Encouraged by our findings he scheduled a trip to Ethiopia with his wife, Jeni, in December.

Ziway, hardly a resort town, offers only the most basic accommodations. We didn't get very luxurious rooms at our $4 a night hotels, but Ed and Jeni were good sports about it for the five days of their visit. And, even though the restaurants listed many choices on their menus, it seemed they never had the food we wanted to order.

When we two American couples met with the MKC elders in that same simple, cramped meeting room, they again laid out their vision for the benefit of Ed and Jeni. It included the same priorities they had told Peggy and me in our prior visit, but with special emphasis on building the bridge over the river to get to Bochessa. At one point Ed interrupted, "I build group homes for orphans; I do not build bridges." He expressed his desire to visit Bochessa and the sites the village offered for his work, be it a group home or projects beyond that.

This time we experienced firsthand the real dangers of crossing the river. The river was at its peak, and the makeshift bridge of eucalyptus poles had been swept away by the stream. The river was approximately one-third kilometer (one-quarter mile) wide. Rowboats with young boys at the oars provided the only means for crossing. It was an interesting adventure for us, but for the people of Bochessa it was a daily reality and a dangerous one, at that.

Somewhat unsteadily we got into a rickety boat, and a young boy rowed us across the river. Without the burden of OSHA (Occupational Safety and Health Administration—a federal agency of the United States) standards or other governmental regulations, our young captains provided no life preservers or other safety measures. Several Ethiopians rode in the boat with us, most carrying a wide array of goods, including one bicycle. A schoolboy in the boat beside ours unexpectedly fell out, losing his books and school supplies to the bottom of the churning river. His boat mates quickly fished him back into their boat, but he was very upset over losing his school books.

We safely crossed the river, and as we climbed up the opposite bank, a large crowd of Bochessa residents greeted us. We were not expecting this welcome. Lined up sitting on the grass, they had waited a long time for our arrival.

One by one the village elders and leaders stood and told us the burdens of their hearts. Not only did they need an orphanage, school, and clinic, but a bridge over that river concerned them most.

One told a story of a pregnant woman trying to cross the river to give birth in Ziway and being swept away.

Another described the difficulties of trying to transport grain, sheep, and wares to market on the rickety boats.

A man fortunate enough to have a bicycle still had the challenge of loading it on a rowboat to continue his trip to Ziway.

School kids needed to cross the river each day, both ways, on those boats, and they were always in danger of falling out, just as we had witnessed in the boat next to ours.

With a great deal of respect and patience, we listened to their stories and pleas. In the end, Ed, touched deeply by the sincerity and passion of their request, told the crowd he would go back to the U.S. and try to raise funds for the bridge. A titter of excitement raced through the crowd.

Following that meeting we moved on to tour the three pieces of property (each over two hectares, or five acres) being offered to us. After an emotionally and physically exhausting day we slept well that night in our cut-rate hotel rooms, oblivious to the honking horns, cockroaches, and mosquitoes.

After we left Ziway and returned to Addis Ababa, Ed, Jeni, Peggy, and I decided we had better start doing our homework on building bridges. Not knowing where else to start, we called Tsion and Eshetu's son, Yonas, the architect who had designed the group home for children in Addis Ababa for us.

Yonas reminded me, "Gary, I'm an architect, not an engineer. And I know nothing about designing bridges. However, I used to have a professor at Addis Ababa University who is a famous bridge engineer. I think he's retired now, but maybe he can help you or can direct you to someone who can. His name is Negussie Tebedge."

"Thanks, Yonas, that gives us something to start with. Can you give me his mobile number?"

That being the Schwartzes' final day in Ethiopia, I figured I had nothing to lose by calling Professor Negussie.

I explained who I was and the reason for my calling him out of the blue.

He replied, "I'm interested. When should we meet?"

"Well, the sponsors of the bridge are in Addis now, but they are leaving tonight to go back to America. Would it be possible to meet at noon for lunch?"

"Sure; where?"

"What about the Cloud 9 Restaurant in the Getu Building? Will that work for you?" The Getu Building is a very modern, impressive high-rise building on Bole Avenue, the street that is the location of choice for progressive, forward-looking businesses.

"Good choice. I designed that building, so I know right where Cloud 9 is."

I whispered to myself, "Thank you, Lord, for putting that suggestion in my head."

When I shook hands with Professor Negussie something struck me that this might be the famous engineer who had just been called on to solve a serious dilemma I had read about in the newspaper.

The Ethiopia Electric Power Corporation, the government-owned monopolistic electric utility, was in the process of building a huge hydroelectric plant in southern Ethiopia. A tremendously heavy piece of electrical generating equipment had just arrived from Turkey and was being delivered to the construction site. When the truck carrying it arrived at the bridge over the Awash River, someone calculated this piece of equipment weighed three times the capacity of the bridge. Unfortunately, that lack of forward planning is not atypical for Ethiopia.

The power company called Professor Negussie for help. In the end he designed a twenty-two-axle trailer (four wheels on each axle) pulled by two semi-tractors. That's a total of 108 tires. His goal was to spread the tremendous weight over as long a span as possible. As that semi-tractor-trailer combination drove onto the bridge, two very heavily weighted trucks were on the opposite end of the bridge. As the rig passed the midpoint of the bridge, those heavy trucks drove off and two other heavily loaded trucks rolled onto the end of the bridge which the rig had just passed. These heavy trucks at each end counterbalanced the weight of the rig as it entered and left the bridge.

I asked Professor Negussie, "Are you, by any chance, the engineer who designed the rig to transport that electrical transformer across the Awash River bridge?"

His eyes lit up. "Yes, that was me. Here, take a look at this." Obviously pleased to be recognized for that engineering masterpiece, he dived into his bag and pulled out a video camera and played for me the crossing of the big rig over the bridge.

I asked him, "How confident were you that the bridge wasn't going to collapse into the river?"

"Didn't you see where I was taking the video from?"

"Yes, it looks like you were standing right in the middle of the bridge." That had to be the case, since I noticed the video showed the rig entering from his left, passing in front of him, and exiting to his right.

"Offering to stand in the middle of the bridge while the rig passed over was the only way I could convince the others that I knew what I was doing and that I believed in my calculations!"

Our small bridge project seemed like a cakewalk to Negussie in comparison to the Awash River bridge challenge he had just described. He listened to our story and our vision for the Bochessa River. At the conclusion he not only expressed deep interest in engineering our bridge, but he also said he wanted to do it for free! And he did, saving us many dollars.

Shortly after returning to the U.S., Ed reported he had raised the funds. We could start the work!

Prior to Professor Negussie's designing of the bridge, though, we had to hire highway engineers to determine the topography of the area and pinpoint the bridge's exact location. Professor Negussie took that topographical data and designed the bridge. Upon receiving the bridge blueprints we solicited bids from four engineers to actually build the bridge. After evaluating their proposals we selected the engineer for the construction, which began in June 2009.

And once again, I had to ask, "Lord, I'm just an Illinois farm boy. What do I know about building a bridge out here in rural Ethiopia?"

And He seemed to whisper to me, "Not only a bridge, but I have other jobs lined up for you."

That revelation cemented our commitment to God and to our new friends at Ziway that we would move to Ziway during the next few months to take up our new work.

CHAPTER 31

Misgana Ministries

We resigned from the Korean Hospital at the end of December 2008, the same month Ed and Jeni Schwartz visited Ethiopia and committed to build the bridge at Bochessa. We foresaw a period of time in front of us during which we would not be engaged full-time with development projects. Peggy and I wondered how God desired we should spend our time prior to taking up full-time work in Ziway.

Just before our departure from the Korean Hospital, we "by chance" met Marku and Kati, Finnish friends of ours, in the hospital corridor. We had originally met Marku and Kati eight years earlier in Amharic language school.

We were shocked to see each other. We thought they had moved back to Finland, and they had no idea what had happened to us. Marku, like Peggy, was not enamored with studying languages. But, amazingly, he reported that both he and Kati had reenrolled at the same language school, and it was much better this time around. The teaching method was more conversation-based, rather than grammar-based. He oozed enthusiasm talking about his Amharic studies.

That report inspired Peggy to give Amharic school another try. I was extremely happy to join her to improve my Amharic proficiency also. So, we enrolled in the same school we had studied at eight years earlier. We thought this would be a good opportunity, also, for God to more clearly unveil His plans for us. It would allow us to put our affairs in order for construction of the bridge and our move to Ziway.

Some of the same teachers from eight years before continued to teach at the school, so it created no small stir for them to see us back as students. We studied Amharic from January to May, although with a short interruption to travel back to the U.S. for the birth of our second grandchild in March.

Although very occupied with studies, our time as students allowed us more freedom to focus on our future. During this interval we worked with the engineers for the bridge and arranged for its construction.

Our decision to move our home to Ziway was reinforced as we saw God's plans for us come into sharper focus. We contracted with a builder in Ziway who had a simple, but comfortable, house under construction. Although the house was quite small, he had intentionally designed it for the lifestyle of Westerners, i.e., with an indoor kitchen and indoor bathrooms. With our paying twenty-two months of rent in advance, he was able to finish the house for us in July. We moved to Ziway on July 23, just as the two-year lease on our house in Addis Ababa expired. This is the house we had rented during the Ethiopian millennium frenzy. Since we had committed to Mr. Moon that we would work at the Korean Hospital for up to two years, we had signed a two-year lease on our house. The timing was miraculous.

After hearing about our new vision, other interested sponsors from America approached us with ideas for development work they were interested in. Along with a school in Ziway, we suggested they help with a feeding program for the students, a home for street kids, finishing the construction of the new church building, reopening a nursery school in the neighboring town of Adami Tulu, and starting a home for orphans in Adami Tulu.

As God revealed these projects to us, along with the corresponding sponsors, we started to grasp the tremendous potential for the vision Temesgin had more than a year before for an integrated rural development project. It could include all kinds of things in addition to what had already been proposed—farming, gardening, micro-loans, women's cooperatives, livestock, chickens; there were limitless possibilities for developing this rural community.

Peggy and I decided that since our development project was taking on an identity of its own, it should have a name. After much discussion and thought, we decided to name it "Misgana Ministries." In Amharic, misgana means "praise" or "thanksgiving."

Where will Misgana Ministries lead us? We have no idea. After all, I'm simply an Illinois farm boy, and what do I know about any of this? But we will trust in God, having faith that He has brought us this far via some very unexpected and amazing circumstances and relationships, and He will continue to direct our paths.

CHAPTER 32

Our Support Team

The story of my missionary journey would not be complete without a few words about the wonderful team that has faithfully stood beside Peggy and me through all of its unexpected twists and turns.

For us, as for most new missionaries, the thought of serving in a poverty-ridden country, malarial steaming jungle, or frigid arctic waste did not frighten us nearly as much as the thought of asking others to give money towards our support. Even the thought of asking humbled me to the borderline of fear.

My parents raised me to be independent, and I have always sought independence. I don't relish the thought of having to ask others for help. As Y2K approached, I spent considerable time, energy, and dollars to get ready. Our family stashed away food, dug a well, stored up gasoline, bought a generator, and did many other things to prepare for the Millennial Meltdown.

But God, with His divine sense of humor, led us in February 2000 to become overseas missionaries just after we survived the puffball that Y2K turned out to be. Many things loomed larger than life over Peggy and me when we made that fateful decision to cast our lot with Wycliffe Bible Translators. I went from preparing to be as independent as I could possibly be to facing the humiliation of asking family and friends to send in money so we could buy our daily bread.

Wycliffe Bible Translators provided us with a lot of training regarding "partnership development," as they called it. Whatever fancy package you put it in, it is still "asking for money," not an attractive idea to most people. Wycliffe asked us to make a list of anyone we could think of who might be a financial or prayer supporter. They suggested that list should be no fewer than 300 names, and 500 would be better. That seemed an almost unachievable goal for us.

In the end we put together a list of nearly 400 names and addresses. Wycliffe gave us guidelines for writing a letter inviting the people on our list to come aboard our missionary support team. We wrote the letter, and while in Colorado on "vacation" we wrote personal notes on each one, prayed over them, and sent them off. And as reported previously, the results were overwhelming and humbling.

During our training in Dallas our teachers and advisors told us that even though a missionary has good initial momentum, it takes a lot of work to maintain it. Supporters themselves run into financial difficulty; a family member or close friend becomes a missionary and "your" missionary dollars go to them; supporters die; they lose interest; and any number of other things can happen to diminish financial support.

We heard every horror story imaginable, including one of a missionary family who relied on only one church for all its support. The church split, their missionary support dried up, and the family ended up stranded in a remote country with no money to get back home. Others received negative monthly financial statements after their car insurance, medical insurance, furlough fund, taxes, and other deductions were subtracted from their income. Still others had to be sent home early by their branch offices because their support had fallen to such a low level they were not able to support themselves. Instead of helping, they created a burden on the branch office.

We certainly couldn't bear the thought of any of those things happening to us, even though they easily could. One old retired South American missionary in the local Wycliffe regional office in Dallas sent around a note announcing her availability for counseling on partnership development. I made an appointment to see her. During our meeting we discovered that not many people were taking advantage of her offer (much to their peril, I later realized).

She gave us creative ideas for preparing newsletters, bulletins, and year-end "annual reports." All that information proved valuable; however, I will always remember the emotion in her voice when she emphasized, "If your supporters don't hear from you, they will forget you! Never assume that that generous stream of contributions will go on forever."

We haven't forgotten that advice. From that point on we have sent a monthly e-mail newsletter to all our supporters and anyone who asks to be added to our list. Sometimes even I cannot predict what I will write about each month until the words start going down on the computer screen. I try my best not to make it the predictable "missionary newsletter," but rather write about an engaging topic that will attract the reader's imagination and keep his interest.

In a recent six-month period I not only wrote about our move to Ziway, the projects we had underway, and this book-writing project, but also tied in the lack of availability of Coca-Cola in Ethiopia, an illegal left turn I made that resulted in a friendship with a cop, trying to determine the sex of turtles, and my views on attempting to live peacefully with our Muslim neighbors.

This method of topic selection must be working to some extent, as our e-mail list continues to grow. We have people on the list whom we have never met. We also hear about people who forward our newsletters on to their own list of addressees. And that is fine with us. We have people of all kinds of religious (including Muslim), ethnic, and social backgrounds receiving our newsletter each month. As far as we are concerned the further God's Word and news of His work spreads, the better. We now consider raising the awareness level of the plight of poor people and unsaved people one of our outreaches. So many people in the developed world are simply not aware of how other people around the world struggle to survive and that many have never heard the gospel of Jesus Christ—or even heard of Jesus, for that matter.

Originally we sent out a quarterly paper newsletter by postal mail. As people acclimated to e-mail and its ability to transmit information almost instantaneously, we cut our paper letters back to three times a year. Eventually we dialed that down to twice a year. Some people wonder why we even send out a postal newsletter. That is a good question; however, it seems to be impor-tant to occasionally give our team something to hold in their hands and, if they wish, to keep record of our contact information in a more permanent form. In addition, we have a substantial number of supporters who don't use e-mail.

In my tenure as administrator of the SIL Addis Ababa branch, I helped prepare the annual SQW (Support Quota Worksheet) for the branch members. If we noticed a member slipping in his finan-cial support, most of the time it could be tied back to lack of com-munication with his support team. Sometimes missionaries of other organizations complained that their support had shrunk to a dangerously low level, causing them to make an unplanned trip home for a fund-raising tour. If I asked them when they sent out their last newsletter, they typically responded that it had been a long time ago.

We are very thankful for the faithfulness and generosity of our supporters. Because our denomination, at the time we left for the mission field, did not support the sending of foreign missionaries, we obviously could not ask the denomination or local churches for support funds. And, due to the conservative stance of the denomi-nation against "co-mingling of the faiths," we weren't allowed to go to the Presbyterian, Baptist, or Assemblies of God church down the street and ask for support. Our only alternative was to find support from individuals, which turned out to be a huge blessing.

We envied other missionaries who simply had spoken to three, four, or five churches and raised their quota of support. When the subject of financial support came up in discussions with our missionary friends, the conversation often turned to "how many supporting churches do you have?" Our cohorts always seemed shocked when we said "none." They surely must have wondered what kind of backslidden heathens we were, not to have a single supporting church, but that was the truth until just recently. All our support came from individuals.

In recent years our home congregation began supporting us with some financial gifts. So now we can say we do have one supporting church.

In our transitions from Wycliffe to Project Mercy and from Project Mercy to Loving Shepherd, we are confident that all our supporters stayed loyal to us. We praise God for that. When people tell us they will continue to support us in our new work because they have faith in us and what we are doing, we are deeply humbled, yet find tremendous gratification in that.

Another wonderful blessing we discovered for having a support team made up exclusively of individuals is all the other ways they help us. We know a large percentage of the team pray for us, often on a daily basis, and that reassures and encourages us. Prayer for missionaries living and working in foreign countries among unfamiliar cultures is vital. Others help in countless other ways. To try to list those ways would single out some friends and leave out others. I will simply reiterate that we have been blessed beyond measure by our support team.

And we know that the Holy Spirit is the One prompting their charity towards us. When our financial needs increase, without any communication from us our support funds go up. When the need diminishes, the amount of support we receive goes back down. I keep records of every donation we have ever received. As I look back over the years I see an increase in our support during the times we had to pay tuition for Sam at Rift Valley Academy and when we needed to buy airline tickets to the States.

God is good, and He is in control.

Peggy and I have gone from trying to rely solely on ourselves to relying much more on Him. Each passing year we observe with confidence that our Lord brought us through it, and this fuels our confidence that He will also be with us going forward.

CHAPTER 33

Conclusion

Even though I feel I am simply an Illinois farm boy, God has led me down interesting and amazing paths I could never have even dreamed about back when I really was an Illinois farm boy. Perhaps the journey from high school to college to army to graduate school to State Farm Insurance was predictable. After all, the University of Illinois is only one hour from my boyhood home. Purdue University is about three hours away, and State Farm's corporate headquarters is only about forty-five minutes away. Ft. Sam Houston and Ft. Hood, both in Texas, are over twenty hours away, but still not outside the realm of imagination, especially since Uncle Sam had an insatiable appetite for drafting young men into the military just at the time I was an eligible candidate.

But all the other places on the four continents I subsequently visited could not have been predicted. And, for sure, no one could have ever predicted I would work in Africa, as an administrator for work in Bible translation, as a hospital administrator, and in starting up, in partnership with my bride, an integrated rural development project.

In 2000, the same year Peggy and I made the decision to become overseas missionaries, Dr. Bruce Wilkinson published a little book called The Prayer of Jabez: Breaking Through to the Blessed Life (Multnomah Books, 2000).

The book is based on the passage from 1 Chronicles 4:10, which reads, "Jabez called on the God of Israel, saying, Oh that you would bless me indeed, and enlarge my border, and that your hand might be with me, and that you would keep me from evil, that it not be to my sorrow! God granted him that which he requested" (WEB).

Jabez's prayer reveals that he understood what many people in his day and even today do not understand. God wants to bless our lives. But God will not do that without our permission. We have to ask Him to do so. God also wants to increase our sphere of influence for Him. He wants us to step out in faith boldly. In order to increase our influence for God we have to ask God to enlarge our "borders" or our "territory."

Next, we should desire a close relationship with God, a daily walk with Him. That is, we should ask Him that His "hand might be with me." Evil is painful, not only to ourselves, but also to our God. In the New International Version Jabez asks God, "Let your hand be with me, and keep me from harm." We as humans like neither pain nor harm. We, like Jabez, need to pray that the Lord will keep us from both. As a matter of fact He is the only one who can reliably do so.

Then, most importantly, we read that God heard Jabez's prayer, approved it, and granted Jabez's wishes. To be clear, I am not suggesting or endorsing the "name it, claim it" or "prosperity" gospel. Instead, I am digging deep into the actual context of this passage. Jabez is similar to the Hebrew word for "pain," and in the preceding verse (verse 9), Jabez's mother said, "I gave birth to him [Jabez] in pain" (NIV). There is nothing to suggest ease or comfort surrounding Jabez's circumstances.

But, just as Jabez did, we need to cry out to God; we need to make our impassioned pleas. God wants to hear our prayers.

I read Dr. Wilkinson's book and felt convinced that he was relaying a special message to me. Since reading the book I have prayed the prayer of Jabez every day. And as I examine each of the four parts of Jabez's prayer, I see where God has answered each in my life, too.

I have been blessed with friends, acquaintances, work, travel, and experiences beyond anything I could have imagined in 2000 or prior. Obviously, my territory (borders) has expanded beyond comprehension. I am now more familiar with events in Africa than those in my own country. I have been to parts of the world out of the league of an Illinois boy.

Peggy and I have been exposed to many unusual circumstances, dangers of all types, and surrounded by diseases (not only pestilences such as malaria and cholera, but also the vast array of diseases we encountered in the two hospitals we worked in for nearly six years), but to this point God has seen us safely through.

And God has kept me from evil. Not that I am without sin; I confess that I am a sinner, a fallen man living in the flesh, cursed with the sin nature of Adam and sinning daily. But concerning the sins that would sidetrack my career, put my family at risk, or bring shame to myself or others, God has been good to me. He has preserved me and kept me from being harmed.

Essentially, the Lord has turned my world upside down as I have traveled this missionary journey of mine. Prior to being turned upside down I had been looking at the world from the wrong perspective, relying on my own efforts. Only when I had to give up everything I so strongly relied upon myself to provide did I find the true self that God intended for me to be and His purpose for me.

Chuck Colson wrote in his book Loving God (Zondervan, 1996),

It is not what we do that matters, but what a sovereign God chooses to do through us. God doesn't want our success; He wants us. He doesn't demand our achievements;

He demands our obedience. The kingdom of God is a kingdom of paradox, where through the ugly defeat of a cross, a holy God is utterly glorified. Victory comes through defeat; healing through brokenness; finding self through losing self.

Of course, our success-mad, egocentric culture cannot grasp that crucial truth. It is understandable only when the false values that obsess us are stripped away, sometimes in the midst of our most abject failures. Surely that was so in my life.

Amen. And that is how God can take an Illinois farm boy and ship him off to Africa to be used in His kingdom.

We all have talents that God has given us, talents that He wants us to use in His service. He's waiting for us to submit to Him and stop relying on ourselves. He has a better, more interesting career in store for us. Unfortunately, we too often respond to Him with excuses that someday will sound feeble, pathetic, and unconvincing when we stand before Him.

In His Word on several occasions, directly from the mouth of His Son, God gives us marching orders regarding what He expects of us. One example is "Therefore go and make disciples of all nations, baptizing them in the name of the Father and of the Son and of the Holy Spirit, and teaching them to obey everything I have commanded you" (Matthew 28:19-20 NIV).

Just before He departed from earth to return to heaven, Jesus gave us this command. Whenever we are about to depart from our loved ones, whether it be on a journey or in death, we save our most heartfelt wishes and requests for last, hoping that these are the words that will be long remembered by those we are leaving. The words quoted above from the book of Matthew were Jesus' final words before leaving His disciples. They are important. He really meant them. They are His desire for us. We cannot ignore them.

My overriding purpose for writing this book is to encourage

you, the reader, not to ignore Jesus' impassioned plea. Perhaps the path looks too difficult or too uncertain or filled with too much sacrifice. Or, perhaps, you feel you don't have the training or knowledge necessary. Or you may feel that missionary life is only for those with a special calling or God-given talents that you don't have.

I understand, because I have been there. I ask you to simply submit yourself to God, and He will take over from there.

I know. Because if an Illinois farm boy can do it, anyone can do it.

Praise be to God and to our Savior, the Lord Jesus Christ!

How to Contact the Author

By Email:
gary.peggyifft@yahoo.com

By Postal Mail in Ethiopia:
Gary Ifft
P. O. Box 27531-1000
Addis Ababa, Ethiopia

How to Connect with Misgana Ministries

Learn more about the work of Misgana Ministries in Ethiopia by contacting them through any of the following means:

By Postal Mail to Contact the U.S. office of Misgana Ministries:
Misgana Ministries
711 Thistlewood CC Ct.
Normal, IL 61761
U.S.A.

Website:
www.misganaministries.org

Misgana Ministries U.S. Office Telephone Number:
309-530-9241

By Email:
hodelrh@gmail.com